ISBN 978-1-331-11707-0
PIBN 10147099

1 MONTH OF
FREE
READING

at

www.ForgottenBooks.com

By purchasing this book you are eligible for one month membership to ForgottenBooks.com, giving you unlimited access to our entire collection of over 1,000,000 titles via our web site and mobile apps.

To claim your free month visit:

www.forgottenbooks.com/free147099

English
Français
Deutsche
Italiano
Español
Português

www.forgottenbooks.com

Mythology Photography **Fiction**
Fishing Christianity **Art** Cooking
Essays Buddhism Freemasonry
Medicine **Biology** Music **Ancient**
Egypt Evolution Carpentry Physics
Dance Geology **Mathematics** Fitness
Shakespeare **Folklore** Yoga Marketing
Confidence Immortality Biographies
Poetry **Psychology** Witchcraft
Electronics Chemistry History **Law**
Accounting **Philosophy** Anthropology
Alchemy Drama Quantum Mechanics
Atheism Sexual Health **Ancient History**
Entrepreneurship Languages Sport
Paleontology Needlework Islam
Metaphysics Investment Archaeology
Parenting Statistics Criminology
Motivational

ALTA CALIFORNIA:

EMBRACING NOTICES OF THE

CLIMATE, SOIL, AND AGRICULTURAL PRODUCTS

OF

NORTHERN MEXICO

AND

THE PACIFIC SEABOARD;

ALSO, A HISTORY OF THE

𝔐𝔦𝔩𝔦𝔱𝔞𝔯𝔶 𝔞𝔫𝔡 𝔑𝔞𝔳𝔞𝔩 𝔒𝔭𝔢𝔯𝔞𝔱𝔦𝔬𝔫𝔰 𝔬𝔣 𝔱𝔥𝔢 𝔘𝔫𝔦𝔱𝔢𝔡 𝔖𝔱𝔞𝔱𝔢𝔰 𝔡𝔦𝔯𝔢𝔠𝔱𝔢𝔡 𝔞𝔤𝔞𝔦𝔫𝔰𝔱 𝔱𝔥𝔢 𝔗𝔢𝔯𝔯𝔦𝔱𝔬𝔯𝔦𝔢𝔰 𝔬𝔣 𝔑𝔬𝔯𝔱𝔥𝔢𝔯𝔫 𝔐𝔢𝔵𝔦𝔠𝔬,

IN THE YEAR 1846—'47.

WITH

DOCUMENTS DECLARATORY OF THE POLICY OF THE PRESENT ADMINIS-
TRATION OF THE NATIONAL GOVERNMENT IN REGARD
TO THE ANNEXATION OF CONQUERED TERRITORY
TO THIS UNION,

AND THE

OPINION OF THE HON. JAMES BUCHANAN ON THE WILMOT PROVISO, &c.

BY A CAPTAIN OF VOLUNTEERS.

PHILADELPHIA:
H. PACKER & CO., PUBLISHERS.
SOLD BY THE BOOKSELLERS GENERALLY.
1847.

PREFACE.

————

THE writer believes this work to be *worth its price,* and *a perusal;* but he hopes that no thinking citizen will *take his word* for the latter averment—and that all will believe the first.

WASHINGTON, D. C., *September,* 1847.

CONTENTS.

CHAPTER I.

Alta California—Its Extent, &c.—Beja California—Bays and Harbours of Alta California—Climate, Soil, and Agricultural Productions, &c. 9

CHAPTER II.

The Designs of the Government at Washington—Mr. Secretary Bancroft's Instructions to Captain Sloat, in 1845—Same in 1846—Confidential Communication of Mr. Secretary Marcy to General Kearny—Letter of Instruction addressed by Mr. Bancroft to Captain Sloat, after the Battles of Palo Alto and Resaca de la Palma, &c. 13

CHAPTER III.

Justification of War—The Motives of the Government at Washington Reviewed—Report of the Secretary of War in reference to the Occupation of California—Lieut. Col. John C. Fremont—His Revolutionary Movements—The Responsibility of the United States Government, &c. 17

CHAPTER IV.

Report of Captain Sloat—His Proclamations—California Volunteers, &c. 23

CHAPTER V.

Captain Stockton's Communication to the Government at Washington—His Proclamation to the People of Alta California—His Ordinance—Government, &c. 27

CHAPTER VI.

Mr. Secretary Bancroft's Communication to Captain Sloat, of the 12th of July, 1846—Do. of the 17th of August—General Scott to General Kearny—Mr. Secretary Mason to Captain Stockton—Stevenson's Expedition—General Kearny's Operations in California, &c. **30**

CHAPTER VII.

Differences between General Kearny and Captain Stockton—Captain Stockton's Report—Lieut. Col. Fremont's Treaty—Letter of late U. S. Consul—Lieutenant Talbot's Letter—Lieut. Col. Fremont's Explanation—Letter from Mr. Secretary Marcy to General Kearny, &c. **41**

CHAPTER VIII.

General Scott's Letter to Captain Tompkins—Stevenson's Commission actually void—Mr. Secretary Marcy to J. D. Stevenson—A Glance at Mexico—Its People and its Government—Her Future Prospects as a Nation—Texas and Slavery, &c. **49**

CHAPTER IX.

Opinion of the Hon. James Buchanan of the Wilmot Proviso—His Appeal to the Democracy of Pennsylvania—The Question of Slavery in California Reviewed—36° 30', or the Missouri Compromise—The policy of the South, and the motive for a Slave Market—Emigrants to California and Northern Mexico. **56**

ALTA CALIFORNIA.

CHAPTER I.

Alta California—Its extent, &c.—Baja California—Bays and harbours of Alta California—Climate, Soil, and Agricultural Productions, &c.

THE extent of country embraced in the territory of *Alta California*, is bounded north by the 42° of north latitude, and extends south very near to the 32° ; on the west it is bounded by the Pacific Ocean, and extends east from the shores of the Pacific a distance of near 1000 miles. Its area, according to Mexican authorities, is 376,344 square miles; and its population is estimated at 25,000.

Baja California is comprised in the peninsula of California. This has an extent of about 800 miles from north to south, and a breadth varying from 60 to 250 miles, and an estimated area of 57,021 square miles, and a population of 13,419.

The two Californias embrace a sea-coast, on the Pacific and Gulf of California, over 2,500 miles in extent, and include the only good harbours of Mexico, and decidedly the best for commerce on the Pacific. San Francisco, Monterey, Santa Barbara, Buenaventura, San Gabriel, and San Diego, are safe harbours, and afford good anchorage for shipping. These are all within Alta California; and there are as many equally advantageous sea-ports in Baja California.

For soil, climate, and capacity for husbandry, the territories of California are not inferior to any other portion of America; and let Sonora and Chihuahua be included, and, for extent of country, it is the best, for agricultural purposes and for commerce, of the world. Yet it must not be supposed that California is without its drawbacks, which indolent and unfortunate settlers will be sure to notice. (1) In such an extent of country as the Californias embrace, there must necessarily exist a variety of soil as well as of climate ; (2) and as, upon the Pacific coast, latitude does not determine the climate nor govern the productions of the soil, (3) the climate, soil, and productions of all Northern Mexico may be regarded as similar, subject only to the variations produced by difference of elevation. Such is the magnificence of the countries which have been seized by the orders of the government at Washington, *as a conquest of the people of the United States;* and it is intimated that the President claims to include in the conquest not only the two Californias and New Mexico, but Sonora and Chihuahua; which, with the Californias and New Mexico, embrace over one-third of the entire territory of the republic of Mexico.

NOTES TO CHAPTER I.

(1.) THE SOIL AND PRODUCTIONS OF CALIFORNIA.
BY A RESIDENT OF TWENTY-TWO YEARS.

Having given some information in one of my former letters of the fertility of the soil in most parts of California, I have to observe that whatever I have mentioned on this head is the result of twenty-two years' experience that I have had in California; and I feel my-self bound, as a lover of truth, to warn all and every person wishing to emigrate to this country, to beware of some pamphlets that have been published, both by Americans and Mexicans, within the last three or four years, concerning the extraordinary fertility of the soil, otherwise, on their arriving here, they may be disappointed.

I was led to mention this warning from having a pamphlet, now before me, written by Don Manuel Castanares, who went to Mexico in the year 1843, as representative of California. This gentleman does not scruple to say, " the land of California is so surprisingly productive, that wheat commonly yields crops of from four hundred to six hundred for one of sowing, and maize or Indian corn from one thousand to twelve hundred bushels for one of seed, and beans from five hundred to seven hundred for one of seed." Now, as I should be very sorry for any family well situated in life to sacrifice their property in America for the purpose of emigrating to California, under the expectation of making an independent fortune in one or two years by agriculture, from having read such a pamphlet as this, which will no doubt find its way to America in a very short time, if it is not already there, I should wish this gentleman, as well as some who have published before him, had been a little more explicit. For instance, if he had said he had seen a grain of wheat yield one thousand or two thousand fold, or a grain of corn yield three thousand fold, or a bean yield three hundred fold,—all these I have seen myself; but still it does not follow that a field sown with either of these different kinds of grain should yield in the same proportion. That the soil would yield, under the hands of an American agriculturist, double the quan-tity of produce from the same quantity of seed it at present yields, I have not the least doubt, but still the account given by Castanares is exaggerated, at the very least, cent. per cent.

Not only this, but all parts of California are not equal in the fertility of soil. To the southward of San Luis Obispo, the farmers consider they have a good crop if they gather thirty bushels for one of seed. Beans, corn, peas, melons, pumpkins, &c.; &c., yield well all over California. * * *

The most beautiful part of California is still occupied by wild Indians. · There are no parts in the settlements, nor in the Sacramento valley, equal to those situated on the west-ern side of the Snowy Mountains. From the head of the river San Joaquin down to the elbow, or, as it is called in Spanish, the *junta*, and on each side of the river *Merced* and the river *Reyes*, lies the most valuable land in California.

From each of these rivers, two of which empty themselves into a lake, produce may be brought into the bay of San Francisco by going to the expense of removing some few im-pediments, which at present exist in the San Joaquin. The lake has an outlet which is a natural canal of about one hundred miles long and about one hundred miles wide, with a constant depth of from twenty-five to thirty feet. It is uniform in all these dimensions from one end to the other, and the current is so trifling that it is almost imperceptible. The reason of this is, that where it enters the San Joaquin, which is at the elbow above men-tioned, the bed of the river is very high, consequently the water cannot run out of the canal so fast as it runs into the lake from three considerable rivers, of which it is formed; and as the high bed of the river prevents the discharge of water from the lake through the canal. In the month of May, June, July and August, the level ground all around the lake, to the distance of eight or ten miles, is all overflown; and then the water is good, as the overflow is occasioned by the melting of the snow in the Snowy Mountains, but in the other months the water of this lake is very brackish and very unwholesome.

On the dryer parts of his immense plain, where the waters which overflow from the lake do not reach, the soil is generally barren, and in some places, for miles and miles, the ground is so soft and light, that, though perfectly dry, a horse will sink up to his knees almost every step; wherever this is the case, the ground is completely barren, bearing nei-ther shrub, bush, tree, nor grass or herbs of any kind. The whole of this valley is pestered with rattlesnakes; so much so, that it is dangerous to be down in the camp on it without taking the precaution to search well to see if there are any holes; and if none are to be seen, it is necessary to drag some brush which may be found on many parts of the plain, where the ground is harder, and with it make a large circular fire, where a person may lie with more safety from these deadly venomous animals. I have been travelling over this plain in hot weather, and for the space of ten miles have seen rattlesnakes as thick as we commonly see ground-squirrels where they are considered plentiful.

This vast plain extends about five hundred miles, running nearly north and south, and may, on an average, be about sixty miles wide; and divides what is called the Great Mountain from the lower range of mountains which run up and down the coast. This lower range of mountains formerly was claimed by the missions in California, and to prevent individuals from obtaining grants of land from the government, about the foot of them every mission established one or more sheep farms, and certainly the climate and the pasture were much adapted to this class of animals, for they increase to an incredible degree. * * *

There are many persons who have tremendous large tracts of beautiful and fertile lands, containing from three to eleven square leagues, and the man who cultivates twenty acres of it without taking the trouble to fence it, is considered among themselves an extraordinarily industrious man, and, at the same time, were it not for the Indians, who work about the farms for little or nothing, (and generally get cheated out of that,) there would be no land cultivated in California; and I have never seen in any part of the country, since the missions have been secularized, a superabundance of provisions, not because the ground will not produce, but because the people are so indolent and careless, that they will not take the trouble to look after it. * * *

In my last, I gave you some account of the manner in which the settlements in California are, and have been for some time past, supplied with horses, and knowing, as I do from experience, the value of this noble animal, and the usefulness of them, in this country in particular, I cannot despatch this article without giving you some information of the reason why there is such a particular necessity for a great number of horses in this country.

In the first place, the whole territory is but very thinly settled; the grants of land which have been given by Mexico are very large, and it is often the case, that a man who lives on a farm will have to travel one or two hundred miles to purchase the actual necessitous clothing, or to sell his produce, which has all, or for the most part, to be carried to market on horseback, on account of the badness of the roads; add to this, that all travelling has to be done on horseback, and as no provender of any kind is laid up by farmers here for winter food, the horses, from September forward, begin to lose their flesh, and by the latter end of November they are scarcely fit to travel at all; consequently, as things now stand, a man who lives a hundred miles from town will need at least ten horses to carry him the journey.

A Californian will never ride a mare, unless he is actually driven to the necessity; he thinks it a disgrace; and some years back, if a Californian had arrived at any farm with a tired horse, and his friend or countryman had offered him a fresh mare, that his own horse might be relieved, and he pursue his journey, he would have looked upon the act as the greatest affront that could be put upon him, and I have many times known a man to defer his journey one or two days rather than ride a mare.

There were originally two distinct breeds of horses in this country, but, for want of care, and curiosity, they have got so crossed and mixed up together, that they are not distinguishable; though I have particularly observed that the best and fleetest, as well as the handsomest horses in this territory, are those which have been caught wild after having come to their growth in the Tular valley. I believe the reason of this to be, those horses which are caught wild have not been injured when very young, as those are which are bred in the settlements and on farms; these are greatly injured when young, by boys, who take every opportunity of driving them into pens to torment them with their lassoes, lashing their legs to throw them, &c., &c., and this is the reason that there are so very few horses of the age of six or seven years that can be found entirely sound.

Then their method of breaking them in likewise tends to break the spirit of the animals, and injure them in their joints. They will take a wild colt and put the saddle on it, and mount it, and ride it down; and when it is tired they take the saddle off it, and make it fast to a post, without any thing to eat, and keep it there for four or five days on nothing but water—saddling it two or three hours each day, at the end of which time they let it go. They are generally two years taming a horse.

(2.) THE VALLEY OF THE GILA.

BY GENERAL KEARNY.

This river, (the Gila,) more particularly the northern side, is bounded nearly the whole distance by a range of lofty mountains; and, if a tolerable wagon road to its mouth from the Del Norte is ever discovered, it must be on the south side. The country is destitute of timber, producing but few cotton-wood and mosquite trees; and, though the soil on the bottom lands is generally good, yet we found but very little grass or vegetation, in consequence of the dryness of the climate and the little rain which falls here. The Pimos Indians, who make good crops of wheat, corn, vegetables, &c., irrigate the land by water from the Gila, as did the Aztecs, (the former inhabitants of the country,) the remains of whose sequias, or little canals, were seen by us, as well as the position of many of their dwellings, and a large quantity of broken pottery and earthenware used by them.

We crossed the Colorado about ten miles below the mouth of the Gila, and, marching near it, about thirty miles further, turned off and crossed the desert—a distance of about sixty miles—without water or grass.

(3.) AGRICULTURAL PRODUCTIONS OF NORTHERN MEXICO.

The chief agricultural productions from the Presidio to Monclova, he says, are corn, sugar, and cotton; of the latter, not much is grown, as there are no gins or factories, and but little demand for it. It grows finely—the stalk being never killed by the cold of winter. It might be profitably cultivated if there was a demand for it.

Sugar grows finely, and only needs a little care and adequate machinery to enable the inhabitants to produce large quantities of it. It is not grained as with us; but, when in syrup, is run into moulds resembling small loaves of loaf sugar, called *pilonces*, weighing about a pound.

Corn grows well and yields abundantly. Two crops of it are made in a year, if the occupant of the ground is not too lazy to tend it. The first is planted in March, and gathered in June and July. The second is planted in July or 1st August, and gathered in November and December. When we arrived at Monclova, the 1st of November, roasting ears and green fodder were abundant for ourselves and horses from the second crop. This is the principal crop of the year, as it is less liable to injury from the vicissitudes of the weather than the first crop. The yield of the corn is about fifty bushels to the acre in a tilled field. With good culture, the quantity would be increased very considerably. The stalks grow to an enormous height. I have seen them often around Monclova so tall, that when sitting on my horse, which is full sixteen hands high, I could not reach the ears of corn.

A well-known physiological fact is continually presented to notice; that is, that latitude alone does not govern the production. Wheat cannot be raised profitably, or of good quality, in Louisiana. Yet here, in latitude 25° and 26°, several hundred miles further south than Louisiana, it is grown to perfection. So are apples and peaches. This is owing to the elevation of the country above the level of the sea.

At Cienegas, a village fifty miles west of Monclova, large quantities of excellent wheat are raised. There are two flouring mills at Monclova, propelled by the stream which passes through the town. The best Mexican flour is not equal in appearance to the American article. It is generally sold without being bolted at all. We used large quantities of this unbolted flour in the army. It makes a very sweet, palatable, and healthy brown bread. It is, however, hard to take down, and the soldiers generally disliked to use it, as they said they did not like to be fed on so much bran so little flour.

The Mexicans keep small sieves in their houses to separate the bran from the flour. It then makes a light bread; and I must say, I have never eaten sweeter or better light bread than is made by the bakers in Monclova and Parras.

Oats and rye are not grown in Mexico. Corn is not generally fed to horses. When they are fed with grain at all, it is usually with barley, which grows finely; but little of it is raised, however.

Nearly all descriptions of vegetables grow finely. With most kinds, a person may select his own time for planting. Fresh peas, lettuce, beans, &c., may be had the year round, by planting them repeatedly. I saw peas six inches in length growing at Parras on the 16th December, which were planted for a winter crop. As the climate is so propitious, and all plants have to be reared by irrigation, a planter or gardener may select his own time for planting.

It might not be profitable to plant corn in the fall; but there is a wide range from February to August to put it into the ground, and still have a good crop.

Oranges grow beautifully and magnificently; but, to our great disappointment, they are all of the sour kind. Sweet oranges are cultivated farther south, and in lower plains and valleys, near the sea-coast.

Pumpkins and a variety of squashes grow abundantly, and are much used. As a general thing, very few vegetables are used by the Mexicans, except red pepper.

CHAPTER II.

The Designs of the Government at Washington—Mr. Secretary Bancroft's Instructions to Captain Sloat in 1845—Same in 1846—Confidential Communication of Mr. Secretary Marcy to General Kearny—Letter of Instruction addressed by Mr. Bancroft to Captain Sloat after the Battles of Palo Alto and Resaca de la Palma, &c.

THE administration of the Government at Washington having failed to maintain the title of the United States to the Territory of Oregon up to 54° 40′, agreeably to the pledges of President Polk and his friends, it seems that their attention, immediately after the settlement of the Oregon question, was turned to the seizure of California and New Mexico, as the means of satisfying those who complained at the dismemberment of Oregon, deeming that the acquisition of 2500 miles of seaboard on the Pacific would be received in full requite for the 9° surrendered to the British government; and particularly so by the people of certain states of the Union who are known to be ever jealous of "the extension of the area of freedom" north of the line adopted by the Missouri compromise; and who are ever looking with a greedy eye to the acquisition of territory, the soil of which is capable of producing a better return for servile labour than the worn-out lands of the Atlantic slave states. The reiterated instructions of the government at Washington to the military and naval officers of the Union are evidences in support of the preceding assumptions. Copies of these are presented to the reader, as they were communicated to Congress by the President; and they very plainly exhibit the fact that the design of the government at Washington, to seize and hold the Californias and New Mexico, was entertained long before the commencement of belligerent operations on the banks of the Rio Grande.

[*Secret and confidential.*]

UNITED STATES NAVY DEPARTMENT, *Washington, June 24, 1845.*

Sir: Your attention is still particularly directed to the present aspect of the relations between this country and Mexico. It is the earnest desire of the President to pursue the policy of peace, and he is anxious that you and every part of your squadron should be assiduously careful to avoid any act which could be construed as an act of aggression.

Should Mexico, however, be resolutely bent on hostilities, you will be mindful to protect the persons and interests of citizens of the United States near your station; and should you ascertain, beyond a doubt, that the Mexican government has declared war against us, you will at once employ the force under your command to the best advantage. The Mexican ports on the Pacific are said to be open and defenceless. If you ascertain with certainty that Mexico has declared war against the United States, you will at once possess yourself of the port of San Francisco, and blockade or occupy such other ports as your force may permit.

Yet, even if you should find yourself called upon, by the certainty of an express declaration of war against the United States, to occupy San Francisco and other Mexican ports, you will be careful to preserve, if possible, the most friendly relations with the inhabitants; and, where you can do so, you will encourage them to adopt a course of neutrality.

Should you fall in with the squadron under Commodore Parker, you will signify to him the wish of the department, that if the state of his vessels will admit of it, he should remain off the coast of Mexico until our relations with that power are more definitively adjusted; and you will take directions from him, as your senior officer, communicating to him these instructions.

The great distance of your squadron, and the difficulty of communicating with you, are the causes for issuing this order. The President hopes most earnestly, that the peace of the two countries may not be disturbed. The object of these instructions is to possess

B

you of the views of the government, in the event of a declaration of war on the part of Mexico against the United States; an event which you are enjoined to do every thing, consistent with the national honour, on your part, to avoid.

Should Commodore Parker prefer to return to the United States, he has permission from the department to do so. In that event, you will command the united squadron. Very respectfully, your obedient servant,   GEORGE BANCROFT.

Com. JOHN D. SLOAT, *Commanding U. S. naval forces in the Pacific.*

UNITED STATES NAVY DEPARTMENT, *Washington,* May 13, 1846.

COMMODORE: The state of things alluded to in my letter of June 24, 1845, has occurred.

You will therefore now be governed by the instructions therein contained, and carry into effect the orders then communicated with energy and promptitude, and adopt such other measures for the protection of the persons and interests, the rights and the commerce of the citizens of the United States, as your sound judgment may deem to be required.

When you establish a blockade, you will allow neutrals twenty days to leave the blockaded ports; and you will render your blockade absolute, except against armed vessels of neutral nations.

Commending you and your ships' companies to Divine Providence, I am, respectfully, your obedient servant,   GEORGE BANCROFT.

Commodore JOHN D. SLOAT, *Commanding U. S. squadron, Pacific.*

UNITED STATES NAVY DEPARTMENT, *Washington,* May 15, 1846.

COMMODORE: By my letter of the 13th instant, forwarded to you through different sources, in triplicate, of which a copy is enclosed, you were informed of the existing state of war between this government and the republic of Mexico, and referred to your instructions bearing date June 24th, 1845, in reference to such a contingency, and directed to "carry into effect the orders then communicated with energy and promptitude, and adopt such other measures for the protection of the persons and interests, the rights and the commerce of the citizens of the United States, as your sound judgment may deem to be required."

I transmit you herewith, by the hands of Midshipman McRae, whom you will employ on your station, a file of papers containing the President's message, and the proceedings of Congress, relative to the existing state of war with Mexico. The President, by authority of Congress, has made proclamation of war between the United States and Mexico. You will find a copy of the proclamation in the papers enclosed.

You will henceforth exercise all the rights that belong to you as commander-in-chief of a belligerent squadron.

You will consider the most important public object to be, to take and to hold possession of San Francisco; and this you will do without fail.

You will also take possession of Mazatlan and of Monterey, one or both, as your force will permit.

If information received here is correct, you can establish friendly relations between your squadron and the inhabitants of each of these three places.

Guymas is also a good harbour, and is believed to be defenceless. You will judge about attempting it.

When you cannot take and hold possession of a town, you may establish a blockade, if you have the means to do it effectually, and the public interest shall require it.

With the expression of these views, much is left to your discretion as to the selection of the points of attack, the ports you will seize, the ports which you will blockade, and as to the order of your successive movements.

A connection between California, and even Sonora, and the present government of Mexico, is supposed scarcely to exist. You will, as opportunity offers, conciliate the confidence of the people in California, and also in Sonora, towards the government of the United States; and you will endeavour to render their relations with the United States as intimate and as friendly as possible.

It is important that you should hold possession, at least, of San Francisco, *even while you encourage the people to neutrality, self-government, and friendship.*

You can readily conduct yourself in such a manner as will render your occupation of San Francisco and other ports a benefit to the inhabitants.

Commodore Biddle has left, or will soon leave, China. If occasion offers, you will send letters for him, to our agent at the Sandwich Islands; conveying to him the wish of the department that he should appear, at once, off California or Sonora.

You will inform the department, by the earliest opportunity, of those ports which you blockade. You will notify neutrals of any declaration of blockade you may make, and give to it all proper publicity. Your blockade must be strict, permitting only armed vessels of neutral powers to enter; but to neutrals already in the ports, you will allow twenty days to leave them.

The frigate "Potomac," and sloop "Saratoga," have been ordered to proceed as soon as possible into the Pacific; and Captain Aulick in the Potomac, and Commander Shubrick in the Saratoga, directed to report to you at Mazatlan, or wherever else they may find your forces. You will do well, if occasion offers, to send orders to Callao and Valparaiso, instructing them where to meet you.

Other reinforcements will be sent you as the exigencies of the service may require.

You will communicate with the department as often as you can, and you will, if practicable, send a messenger with despatches across the country to the Del Norte, and so to Washington. Very respectfully, your obedient servant,

GEORGE BANCROFT.

Commodore JOHN D. SLOAT, *Commanding U. S. naval forces in the Pacific.*

The intentions of the Government at Washington are alike fully expressed in the following copy of a communication from the Secretary of War to General Kearny, containing instructions for the movements he was to lead for the seizure of Alta California.

[*Confidential.*]

WAR DEPARTMENT, *Washington, June 3,* 1846.

SIR,—I herewith send you a copy of my letter to the governor of Missouri for an additional force of 1000 mounted men.

The object of thus adding to the force under your command is not, as you will perceive, fully set forth in that letter, for the reason that it is deemed prudent that it should not, at this time, become a matter of public notoriety; but to you it is proper and necessary that it should be stated.

It has been decided by the President, to be of the greatest importance in the pending war with Mexico, to take the earliest possession of Upper California. An expedition with that view is hereby ordered, and you are designated to command it. To enable you to be in sufficient force to conduct it successfully, this additional force of 1000 mounted men has been provided, to follow you in the direction of Santa Fé, to be under your orders, or the officer you may leave in command at Santa Fé.

It cannot be determined how far this additional force will be behind that designed for the Santa Fé expedition, but it will not probably be more than a few weeks. When you arrive at Santa Fé with the force already called, and shall have taken possession of it, you may find yourself in a condition to garrison it with a small part of your command, (as the additional force will soon be at that place,) and with the remainder press forward to California. In that case, you will make such arrangements, as to being followed by the reinforcements before mentioned, as in your judgment may be deemed safe and prudent. I NEED NOT SAY TO YOU, THAT IN CASE YOU CONQUER SANTA FE, (and with it will be included the department or state of New Mexico,) IT WILL BE IMPORTANT TO PROVIDE FOR RETAINING SAFE POSSESSION OF IT. Should you deem it prudent to have still more troops for the accomplishment of the objects herein designated, you will lose no time in communicating your opinion on that point, and all others connected with the enterprise, to this department. Indeed, you are hereby authorized to make a direct requisition for it upon the governor of Missouri.

It is known that a large body of Mormon emigrants are *en route* to California, for the purpose of settling in that country. You are desired to use all proper means to have a good understanding with them, to the end that the United States may have their co-operation in taking possession of, and holding that country. It has been suggested here, that many of these Mormons would willingly enter into the service of the United States and aid us in our expedition against California. You are hereby authorized to muster into service such as can be induced to volunteer—not, however, to a number exceeding one-third of your entire force. Should they enter the service, they will be paid as other volunteers; *and you can allow them to designate, so far as it can be properly done, the persons to act as officers thereof.* It is understood, that a considerable number of American citizens are now settled on the Sacramento river, near Suter's establishment, called "Nueva Helvetia"—

who are well-disposed towards the United States. Should you, on your arrival in the country, find this to be the true state of things there, you are authorized to organize and receive into the service of the United States such portion of these citizens as you may think useful to aid you to hold the possession of the country. You will, in that case, allow them so *far as you shall judge proper*, to select their own officers. A large discretionary power is invested in you in regard to these matters, as well as to all others in relation to the expeditions confided to your command.

The choice of routes by which you will enter California, will be left to your better knowledge and ampler means of getting accurate information. We are assured that a southern route (called the Caravan route, by which the wild horses are brought from that country into New Mexico) is practicable; and it is suggested as not improbable that it can be passed over in the winter months, or, at least, late in autumn. It is hoped that this information may prove to be correct.

In regard to the routes, the practicability of procuring needful supplies for men and animals, and transporting baggage, is a point to be well considered. Should the President be disappointed in his cherished hope that you will be able to reach the interior of Upper California before winter, you are then desired to make the best arrangement you can for sustaining your forces during the winter, and for an early movement in the spring. Though it is very desirable that the expedition should reach California this season, (and the President does not doubt you will make every possible effort to accomplish this object,) yet, if in your judgment, it cannot be undertaken with a reasonable prospect of success, you will defer it, as above suggested, until spring. You are left unembarrassed by any specific directions in this matter.

It is expected that the naval forces of the United States, which are now, or will soon be, in the Pacific, will be in possession of all the towns on the seacoast, and will co-operate with you in the conquest of California. Arms, ordnance, munitions of war, and provisions, to be used in that country, will be sent by sea to our squadron in the Pacific, for the use of the land forces.

Should you conquer and take possession of New Mexico and Upper California, or considerable places in either, you will establish temporary civil governments therein—abolishing all arbitrary restrictions that may exist, so far as it may be done with safety. In performing this duty, it would be wise and prudent to continue in their employment all such of the existing officers as are known to be friendly to the United States, and will take the oath of allegiance to them. *The duties at the custom-houses ought at once to be reduced to such a rate as may be barely sufficient to maintain the necessary officers without yielding any revenue to the government.* You may assure the people of those provinces that it is the wish and design of the United States to provide for them a free government with the least possible delay, similar to that which exists in our territories. They will then be called on to exercise the rights of freemen in electing their own representatives to the territorial legislature. It is foreseen, that what relates to the civil government will be a difficult and unpleasant part of your duty, and much must necessarily be left to your own discretion.

In your whole conduct you will act in such a manner as best to conciliate the inhabitants, and render them friendly to the United States.

It is desirable that the usual trade between the citizens of the United States and the Mexican provinces should be continued as far as practicable, under the changed condition of things between the two countries. In consequence of extending your expedition into California, it may be proper that you should increase your supply for goods to be distributed as presents to the Indians. The United States superintendent of Indian affairs at St. Louis will aid you in procuring these goods. You will be furnished with a proclamation in the Spanish language, to be issued by you, and circulated among the Mexican people, on your entering into or approaching their country. You will use your utmost endeavours to have the pledges and promises therein contained carried out to the utmost extent.

I am directed by the President to say that the rank of brevet brigadier-general will be conferred on you as soon as you commence your movement towards California, and sent round to you by sea, or over the country, or to the care of the commandant of our squadron in the Pacific. In that way, cannon, arms, ammunition, and supplies for the land forces, will be sent to you.

Very respectfully, your obedient servant,
WILLIAM L. MARCY, *Secretary of War.*
Col. STEPHEN W. KEARNY, *Fort Leavenworth, Missouri.*

The following copy of a communication from the Secretary of the Navy, to the American naval commander on the coast of California, is still more explicit as to the designs of the government at Washington :

UNITED STATES NAVY DEPARTMENT, *Washington, June* 8, 1846.

COMMODORE,—You have already been instructed, and are now instructed, to employ the force under your command, *first, to take possession of San Francisco; next, to take possession of Monterey ; next, to take possession of such other Mexican ports as you may be able to hold ;* next, to blockade as many of the Mexican ports in the Pacific as your force will permit, and to watch over American interests, and citizens and commerce, on the west coast of Mexico.

It is rumoured that the province of California is well disposed to accede to friendly relations with the United States. You will encourage the people of that region to enter into relations of amity with our country.

In taking possession of their harbours, you will, if possible, endeavour to establish the supremacy of the American flag without any strife with the people of California.

The squadron on the east coast of Mexico, it is believed, is in the most friendly relations with Yucatan. In like manner, if California separates herself from our enemy, the central Mexican government, and establishes a government of its own, under the auspices of the American flag, you will take such measures as will best promote the attachment of the people of California to the United States, will advance their prosperity, and will make that vast region a desirable place of residence for emigrants from our soil.

Considering the great distance at which you are placed from the department, and the circumstances that will constantly arise, much must be left to your discretion. You will bear in mind, generally, that this country desires to find in California a friend, and not an enemy ; to be connected with it by near ties; to hold possession of it, at least during the war; and to hold that possession, if possible, with the consent of its inhabitants.

The sloop-of-war "Dale," Commander McKean, sailed from New York, on the 3d instant, to join your squadron. The "Lexington," Lieutenant Bailey, will sail as soon as she can take on board her stores. The "Potomac" and "Saratoga" have also been ordered to the Pacific.

I am, sir, very respectfully, your obedient servant,

GEORGE BANCROFT.

Com. JOHN D. SLOAT, *Com'g U. S. Naval forces in the Pacific ocean.*

CHAPTER III.

Justification of War—The motives of the Government at Washington reviewed—Report of the Secretary of War, in reference to the occupation of California—Lieut. Col. John C. Fremont—His revolutionary movements—The responsibility of the United States government, &c.

THE prosecution of a war by a civilized nation, is understood to be justified only for the purpose of forcing from the opposite belligerent power satisfaction for some national grievance which had been refused, but which was accorded by justice, and demanded by national honour ; and to secure a proper redress for national wrongs, and by inflicting injury and evil upon the government and people of Mexico, to such an extent as should compel them to acknowledge the rights of our citizens, and the justice of the claims of our government has been declared the motives for the prosecution of the existing war with Mexico. If such be the motives of the government at Washington, for which the people of the Union are taxed, and the bones of thousands of American citizens are laid to whiten upon the rocks and sands of Mexico, in the prosecution of the existing war, the instructions given to the American military and naval commanders are in shocking disjoint with the motives of the government. With an intent to do hurt to Mexico and the Mexicans, until they will consent to do us justice, it will be difficult to

3   B 2

discover the policy of the instructions to the commanders charged with the prosecution of the measures of the war, " to conciliate the confidence of the people in California and New Mexico, (territories of Mexico,) towards the government of the United States ; and to render their relations with the United States as intimate and friendly as possible ;" or, " to encourage them to adopt a course of neutrality ;" or, " to encourage the people of that region, (California and New Mexico,) to enter into relations of amity with our country."

Robbery by the footpad is not more heinous than a war prosecuted for conquest. Such a war is but open aggression, and wholesale wrong—embracing all of the individual crimes of robbery, rape, arson and murder. But, if the reading and thinking part of mankind were left to believe the oft repeated declaration of the President of the United States, that the war with Mexico " has not been waged with a view to conquest ;" the fears of the American people would be without cause of excitement, least their country should be made chargeable with the infamy of having prosecuted a war for a conquest, the stupendousness of which might have satisfied an Alexander, a Cæsar, or a Napoleon.

The Secretary of the Navy communicating his instructions to Captain John D. Sloat, commanding the United States squadron on the coast of California, under date of " United States Navy Department, Washington, May 15, 1846," writes as follows :

" *You will consider the most important public object to be,* to take and to hold possession of San Francisco ; and this you will do without fail. You will also take possession of Mazatlan, and of Monterey, one or both, as your force will permit. If information received here is correct, you can establish friendly relations between your squadron and the inhabitants of each of these three places ;" and then the Secretary adds : " *A connection between California, and even Sonora, and the present government of Mexico, is supposed scarcely to exist.*"

The President in a message addressed to Congress, under date of " February 13, 1847," states as follows : " It has been my unalterable purpose, since the commencement of hostilities by Mexico, and the declaration of the existence of war by Congress, to prosecute the war in which the country was unavoidably involved with the utmost energy, with a view to its *speedy and successful termination* by an honourable peace."

The truth of the President's declaration is challenged by facts, and the proceedings of those deriving their authority from him, and acting under his immediate directions. How otherwise, than for the purpose of conquest, could it become " the most important public object," to seize the ports of Alta California, distant 2000 miles, or nearly that, from the theatre of active war, at the very moment when it was supposed by the government at Washington, that " there scarcely existed a connection between California and Sonora, and the government of Mexico ;" and how, with an " unalterable purpose" to prosecute the existing war " with the utmost energy," for the accomplishment of a " speedy and successful termination," could the President have diverted a great portion of the means of the country, and a large and important division of its forces, for the seizure of immense territories, undefended, without forts, and with but a mere nominal white population ; while the divisions of the army actually engaged in the prosecution of the war have been crippled for the want of supplies, and by deficiency of numbers compelled to inactivity, without acknowledging himself criminally weak, or venally false ?

The official instructions of the government at Washington, so plainly expressive of a design to conquer the undefended territories of Alta California, Baja California, New Mexico, and Sonora, given to the American military and naval commanders, seem to have been anticipated, in a measure, in their execution, by other agents who had acted under private instructions; whose operations are thus bluntly explained by the Secretary of War in his official report, under date of December 5, 1846:

"In May, 1845, John C. Fremont, then a brevet captain in the corps of topographical engineers, and since appointed a lieutenant-colonel, left HERE *under orders from this department*, to pursue his explorations in the regions beyond the Rocky Mountains. The objects of this service were, as those of his previous explorations had been, of a scientific character, without any view whatever to military operations. Not an officer or soldier of the United States army accompanied him; and his whole force consisted of sixty-two men, employed by himself for security against Indians, and for procuring subsistence in the wilderness and desert country through which he was to pass.

"One of the objects he had in view, was to discover a new and shorter route from the western base of the Rocky Mountains to the mouth of the Columbia river. This search, for a part of the distance, would carry him through the unsettled, and, afterwards, through a corner of the settled parts of California. He approached these settlements in the winter of 1845-6. Aware of the critical state of affairs between the United States and Mexico, and determined to give no cause of offence to the authorities of the province, with commendable prudence he halted his command on the frontier, one hundred miles from Monterey, and proceeded alone to that city, to explain the object of his coming, to the commandant-general, Castro, and to obtain permission to go to the valley of the San Joaquim, where there was game for his men, and grass for his horses, and no inhabitants to be molested by his presence. The leave was granted: but scarcely had he reached the desired spot for refreshment and repose, before he received information from the American settlements, and by express from our consul at Monterey, that General Castro was preparing to attack him with a comparatively large force of artillery, cavalry, and infantry, upon the pretext that, under the cover of a scientific mission, he was exciting the American settlers to revolt. In view of this danger, and to be in a condition to repel an attack, he then took a position on a mountain overlooking Monterey, at a distance of about thirty miles, intrenched it, raised the flag of the United States, and with his own men, sixty-two in number, awaited the approach of the commandant-general.

"From the 7th to the 10th of March, Lieutenant-colonel Fremont and his little band maintained this position. General Castro did not approach within attacking distance, and Colonel Fremont, adhering to his plan of avoiding all collisions, and determined neither to compromit his government, nor the American settlers, ready to join him at all hazards if he had been attacked, abandoned his position, and commenced his march for Oregon, intending by that route to return to the United States. Deeming all danger from the Mexicans to be passed, he yielded to the wishes of some of his men who desired to remain in the country, discharged them from his service, and refused to receive others in their stead, so cautious was he to avoid doing any thing which would compromit the American settlers, or give even a colour of offence to the Mexican authorities. He pursued his march slowly and leisurely, as the state of his men and horses required, until the middle of May, and had reached the northern shore of the greater Tlamath lake, within the limits of the Oregon Territory, when he found his farther progress in that direction obstructed by impassable snowy mountains and hostile Indians, who had been excited against him by General Castro, had killed and wounded four of his men, and left him no repose either in camp or on his march. At the same time, information reached him that General Castro, in addition to his Indian allies, was advancing in person against him, with artillery and cavalry, at the head of four or five hundred men; that they were passing around the head of the bay of San Francisco to a rendezvous on the north side of it, and that the American settlers in the valley of the Sacramento were comprehended in the scheme of destruction meditated against his own party. Under these circumstances, he determined to turn upon his Mexican pursuers, and seek safety both for his own party, and the American settlers, not merely in the defeat of Castro, but in the total overthrow of the Mexican authority in California, and the establishment of an independent government in that extensive department. It was on the 6th of June, and before the commencement of the war between the United States and Mexico could have been known, that this resolution was taken; and, by the 5th of July, it was carried into effect by a series of rapid attacks by a small body of adventurous men, under the conduct of an intrepid leader, quick to perceive and able to direct the proper measures for accomplishing such a daring enterprise. On the 11th of June, a convoy of 200 horses for Castro's camp, with an officer and fourteen men, were surprised and captured by twelve of Lieutenant-colonel Fremont's party. On the 15th, at daybreak, the military post of Sonoma was surprised and taken, with nine brass cannon, 250 stands of muskets, and several officers, and some men and munitions of war. Leaving a small garrison in Sonoma, Lieutenant-colonel Fremont went to the Sacramento to arouse the American settlers: but scarcely had he arrived there, when an express reached him from the garrison of Sonoma, with information that Castro's whole force was crossing the bay to attack that place. This intelligence was received in the afternoon of the 23d of June, while he was on the American fork of the Sacramento, eighty miles from the little garrison at Sonoma; and, at two o'clock on the morning of the 25th, he arrived at that place with ninety riflemen from the American settlers in that valley. The enemy had not yet appeared. Scouts were sent out to reconnoitre, and a party of twenty fell in with a squadron of seventy dragoons, (all of Castro's force which had crossed the bay,) attacked and defeated it, killing and wounding five, without harm to themselves; the Mexican commander, De la Torre, barely escaping with the loss of his transport boats, and nine pieces of brass artillery, spiked.

"The country north of the Bay of San Francisco being cleared of the enemy, Lieutenant-colonel Fremont returned to Sonoma on the evening of the 4th of July, and, on the morning of the 5th, called the people together, explained to them the condition of things in the province, and recommended an immediate declaration of independence. The declaration was made, and he was selected to take the chief direction of affairs. The attack on Castro was the next object. He was at Santa Clara, an intrenched post on the upper or south side of the Bay of San Francisco, with 400 men and two pieces of field-artillery. A circuit of more than 100 miles must be traversed to reach him. On the 6th of July the pursuit was commenced, by a body of 160 mounted riflemen, commanded by Colonel Fremont in person, who, in three days, arrived at the American settlements on the Rio de los Americanos. Here he learnt that Castro had abandoned Santa Clara, and was retreating south, towards Cuidad de los Angelos, the seat of the governor-general of the Californias, and distant 400 miles. It was instantly resolved on to pursue him to that place. At the moment of departure, the gratifying intelligence was received that war with Mexico had commenced; that Monterey had been taken by our naval forces, and the flag of the United States there raised on the 7th of July; and that the fleet would co-operate with the army against Castro and his forces. The flag of Independence was hauled down, and that of the United States hoisted amidst the hearty greetings, and to the great joy of the American settlers and forces under the command of Lieutenant-colonel Fremont.

"The combined pursuit was rapidly continued; and on the 12th of August, Commodore Stockton and Lieutenant-colonel Frémont, with a detachment of marines from the squadron, and some riflemen, entered the City of the Angels without resistance or objection; the governor-general, Pico, the commandant-general, Castro, and all of the Mexican authorities, having fled and dispersed. Commodore Stockton took possession of the whole country as a conquest of the United States, and appointed Lieutenant-colonel Fremont governor, under the law of nations; to assume the functions of that office when he should return to the squadron."

Lieut. Col. John C. Fremont,* being an officer of the United States government, and operating under the orders of the Secretary of War, must be regarded as having acted in accordance with the instructions and wishes of the government at Washington; and the government could not evade the full responsibility of his whole proceedings, and their effects and consequences, except by a disavowal of his acts, which the government at Washington has not done; but, on the contrary, they have most fully adopted and approved of his measures. Having done this, it is difficult to discover with what motive the Secretary of War has spread out in his report the statement, that "Not an officer or soldier of the United States army accompanied him;" and that "his whole force consisted of sixty-two men, employed by himself for security against Indians, and for procuring subsistence in the wilderness and desert country through which he was to pass." This statement, as an argument, is specious and unbecoming the head of one of the chief bureaus of a great and powerful nation. The persons serving with Lieutenant-colonel Fremont were as emphatically the servants of the United States government as those men who were regularly enlisted in the United States army. Lieutenant-colonel Fremont, holding the commission of the President, in pursuance of the instructions of the War Department, had employed them to assist him in the execution of the orders of the government at Washington—and the people are required to pay them for their services; and while in the service of the United States, whatever may

---

* Lieut. Col. John C. Fremont is a graduate from the Military Academy at West Point, and for several years past has held the post of lieutenant of topographical engineers in the United States army, and in the prosecution of the duties of that office he has made several tours across the Rocky Mountains to the Pacific ocean. He is the son-in-law of the Hon. Thomas H. Benton, senator from the State of Missouri; through whose influence he was promoted, about a year since, to the rank of lieutenant-colonel in the regiment of mounted riflemen. Though quite young for his position in the army, he is accounted a good officer, and a man of considerable talents. He is one of the very few men of genius and science who have been produced at West Point.

Lieutenant-colonel Fremont is understood recently to have returned to the United States from California, under an arrest, ordered by General Kearny on account of some disobedience of the general's orders; the difficulty growing out of the misunderstanding between General Kearny and Captain Stockton, relative to the government of the "conquered territory!" The trial of Lieutenant-colonel Fremont (which it is supposed will take place before the meeting of Congress, in December next,) will, no doubt, elicit many curious facts which the people of the United States must be interested to hear.

have been the terms or conditions of their employment, they were amenable to and governed by the Articles of War; and entitled to the immunities of American soldiers; and they bore the public arms of the United States, and carried on their operations under the flag of the Union. The object of the expedition of Lieutenant-colonel Fremont may be inferred from its acts. It may have intended, and may not have intended services of a "scientific character," as its intentions are altogether immaterial, its acts and measures pursued being alone to be investigated. The Secretary of War by no means gives any unjustifiableness to the conduct of the Mexican general, Castro, in attempting to expel Lieutenant-colonel Fremont and his force from California, by charging that it was done "upon the pretext that, under the cover of a scientific mission, he was exciting the American settlers to revolt," as what the Secretary of War gives information that General Castro charged Lieutenant-colonel Fremont with *intending*, the Secretary also gives information that he *did do*. According to the report of the Secretary of War, Lieutenant-colonel Fremont, with a force, armed and paid by the United States government, entered the territory of Alta California, a province of the Republic of Mexico, and setting the Mexican authorities therein at defiance, seized a position within thirty miles of the principal town, and there formed an intrenchment and hoisted the colours of the United States, on the 7th of March, 1846, thirty-two days before the encounter of the Mexican forces under General Arista, with the American troops commanded by General Taylor; (which occurred on the 8th of May of the same year;) and hence, upon the showing of the Secretary of War, the first belligerent act in this war with Mexico, was executed by the forces of the United States in Alta California, and not by our troops at the meeting of General Taylor with General Arista at Palo Alto, on the banks of the Rio Grande del Norte. The subsequent determination of Lieutenant-colonel Fremont, in the language of the Secretary of War, "not merely to defeat General Castro," but to totally "overthrow the Mexican authority in California, and to establish an independent government in that extensive department," does not vary the first act of aggression, which was executed by an officer of the United States army under the national flag; and the war which was prosecuted by Lieutenant-colonel Fremont, in the gallant manner described by the Secretary of War, was but a continuation of the aggression commenced on the 7th of March, and must be regarded as a part of that transaction. The suggestion that the Californians had declared their independence on the 5th of July, and that Lieutenant-colonel Fremont had acted as the chief of a revolutionary party, and had fought under a revolutionary flag, will only increase the dilemma of those who contend that this war was begun by Mexico; because, while acting under the commission of the President, and receiving pay, according to his commission, from the people of the United States, he could not act under any other authority than that of the government at Washington, or fight under any other flag, except that of the Union, without rendering himself subject to charges for a high offence; and if he carried on war for the United States, under a flag different from that of the Union, he committed an indignity upon the flag of the nation; and if he made war upon his own account, he made himself an outlaw, and as such should have been adjudged and condemned. But the Secretary of War saves Lieutenant-colonel Fremont from all accountability or blame, by assuming his acts as the acts of the government at Washington, and applauding his whole course of conduct; and by this he assumes the responsibility of having commenced, by open acts of aggression committed upon unquestionable territories of Mexico, as well by acts of incitement, the existing war with Mexico; and gives an open and full contradiction to the averments made by the President in his annual message to Congress, in 1846; that, *"Every honourable effort had been used by him to avoid the war which followed,* (his attempt to negotiate—not for peace—but, for the surrender of the Californias, Sonora, and New Mexico,) *but all had proved in vain."*

CHAPTER IV.

Report of Captain Sloat—His Proclamations—California Volunteers, &c,

THE manner in which the designs of the government at Washington have been carried out in Alta California by the United States military and naval commanders, to whom the business of seizing the territory had been confided, is fully exemplified by the following copy of a communication to the government from Capt. John D. Sloat,* late in the command of the United States· naval forces on the coast of California, embracing, with the papers annexed, a report of his proceedings; the originals of which were addressed to the Secretary of the Navy, and the copies furnished by the President to Congress:

FLAG SHIP LEVANT, AT SEA, *July* 31, 1846.

SIR,—I have the honour to report, that on the 7th of June I received, at Mazatlan, information that the Mexican troops, six or seven thousand strong, had by order of the Mexican government invaded the territory of the United States north of the Rio Grande, and attacked the forces under General Taylor, and that the squadron of the United States were blockading the coast of Mexico on the Gulf.

These hostilities I considered would justify my commencing offensive operations on the west coast; I therefore sailed on the 8th, in the Savannah, for the coast of California, to carry out the orders of the Department of the 24th of June, 1845, leaving the Warren at Mazatlan, to bring me any despatches or important information that might reach there. I arrived at Monterey on the 2d of July, where I found the Cyane and the Levant, and learned that the Portsmouth was at San Francisco, to which place they had been previously ordered, to await further instructions.

On the morning of the 7th, having previously examined the defences and localities of the town, I sent Captain Mervine, with the accompanying summons (A), to the military commandant of Monterey, requiring him to surrender the place forthwith to the forces of the United States under my command. At 9 o'clock, A. M., I received his reply (B), stating that he was not authorized to surrender the place, and referred me to the commanding general of California, Don José Castro.

Every arrangement having been made the day previous, the necessary force (about 250 seamen and marines) was immediately embarked in the boats of the squadron, and landed at ten o'clock, under cover of the guns of the ships, with great promptitude and good order, under the immediate command of Captain William Mervine, assisted by Commander H. N. Page, as second.

---

*. Capt. JOHN D. SLOAT, previous to the commencement of the last war with Great Britain, carried on the business of a watch-maker and watch-repairer, in the city of New York. Shortly after the commencement of the war, he gave up his business as a watch-maker, and took to the sea as a privateer's-man; and before the close of the war, he obtained an appointment as a midshipman in the United States navy, and obtaining leave for an immediate examination, he passed the ordeal successfully, and was soon after promoted to the rank of lieutenant. He is now a post-captain of fifteen or sixteen years' standing—and is reputed a good watch-maker. He is understood to be a native of Berkshire county, Massachusetts, and is now, probably, about sixty years of age.

The forces were immediately formed and marched to the custom-house, where my proclamation to the inhabitants of California (C) was read, the standard of the United States hoisted amid three hearty cheers of the troops and foreigners present, and a salute of twenty-one guns fired by all the ships. Immediately afterwards, the proclamation, both in English and Spanish, was posted up about the town, and two justices of the peace appointed to preserve order and punish delinquencies, the alcaldes declining to serve.

Previous to landing, the accompanying general order (D) was read to the crews of all the ships, and I am most happy to state that I feel confident that the inhabitants of Monterey, and of all other places where our forces have appeared, will do them and myself the justice to say that not the least depredation or slightest insult or irregularity has been committed from the moment of our landing until my departure.

Immediately after taking possession of Monterey, I despatched a courier to General Castro, the military commandant of California, with a letter (E), and a copy of my proclamation, to which I received a reply (F). On the 9th, I despatched a letter (G), by courier, to Señor Don Pico, the governor, at Santa Barbara. On the 16th of July, I despatched orders by sea, to Commander Montgomery, to take immediate possession of the Bay of San Francisco, &c., and on the 7th, a duplicate of that order, by land, which he received on the evening of the 8th; and at 7 o'clock, A. M., of the 9th, he hoisted the flag at San Francisco, read and posted up my proclamation, and took possession of that part of the country in the name of the United States.

On the 23d, my health being such as to prevent my attending to so much and so laborious duties, I directed Commodore Stockton to assume the command of the forces and operations on shore; and on the 29th, having determined to return to the United States via Panama, I hoisted my broad pennant on board of the Levant, and sailed for Mazatlan and Panama, leaving the remainder of the squadron under his command, believing that no further opposition would be made to our taking possession of the whole of the Californias, (as General Castro had less than 100 men,) and that I could render much more important service by returning to the United States with the least possible delay, to explain to the government the situation and wants of that country, than I could by remaining in command in my infirm state of health.

Hoping the course I have pursued will meet the approbation of the department, I have the honour to be, most respectfully, your obedient servant, &c.,

JOHN D. SLOAT.

Hon. George Bancroft, *Secretary of the Navy, Washington, D. C.*

(A)—Addressed to "the military commandant at Monterey," under date, "July 7, 1846," and signed "John D. Sloat, Commander-in-chief of the United States naval forces in the Pacific."

Sir,—The central government of Mexico having commenced hostilities against the United States of America, the two nations are now actually at war. In consequence, I call upon you, in the name of the United States of America, to surrender forthwith to the arms of that nation under my command, the forts, military posts, and stations, under your command, together with all troops, arms, munitions of war, and public property of every description under your control and jurisdiction in California.

(B)—Translation of the reply of the military commandant of Monterey, under date of July 7, 1846, signed "Mariana Silva."

The undersigned, captain of artillery in the Mexican army, and military commandant of this port, represents to Señor Commodore of the naval forces of the United States in this bay, that he is not authorized to surrender the place, having no orders to that effect; for the said matter may be arranged by the Señor Commodore with the commandant general, to whom I transmitted the communication delivered to me for the said Señor, the undersigned withdrawing and leaving the town peaceful and without a soldier; nor, according to information from the treasurer, is there any public property or munitions.

(C)—Proclamation of John D. Sloat, commander-in-chief of the United States naval force in the Pacific Ocean, made July 7, 1846.

To the Inhabitants of California:—The central government of Mexico having commenced hostilities against the United States of America, by invading its territory and attacking the troops of the United States stationed on the north side of the Rio Grande, and with a force of 7,000 men under the command of Gen. Arista, which army was totally destroyed, and all their baggage, artillery, &c., captured on the 8th and 9th of May last, by a force of two thousand three hundred men under the command of General Taylor, and the city of Matamoras taken and occupied by the forces of the United States, and the two nations being actually at war by this transaction, I shall hoist the standard of the United States at Monterey, immediately, and shall carry it through California.

· I declare to the inhabitants of California that, although I come in arms with a powerful force, I do not come among them as an enemy to California : on the contrary, I come as their best friend, as henceforward California will be a portion of the United States, and its peaceable inhabitants will enjoy the same rights and privileges they now enjoy, together with the privilege of choosing their own magistrates and other officers, for the administration of justice among themselves, and the same protection will be extended to them as to any other State in the Union.   They will also enjoy a permanent government, under which life, property, and the constitutional right and lawful security to worship the Creator in the way most congenial to each one's sense of duty, will be secured, which, unfortunately, the central government of Mexico cannot afford them, destroyed as her resources are by internal factions, and corrupt officers, who create constant revolutions to promote their own interests and oppress the people.   Under the flag of the United States, California will be free from all such troubles and expense ; consequently, the country will rapidly advance and improve both in agriculture and commerce, as, of course, the revenue laws will be the same in California as in all other parts of the United States, affording them all manufactures and produce of the United States free of any duty, and all foreign goods at one-quarter of the duty they now pay.   A great increase in the value of real estate and the products of California may also be anticipated.

With the great interest and kind feelings I know the government and people of the United States possess towards the citizens of California, the country cannot but improve more rapidly than any other on the continent of America.

Such of the inhabitants of California, whether native or foreigners, as may not be disposed to accept the high privileges of citizenship, and to live peaceably under the government of the United States, will be allowed time to dispose of their property, and to remove out of the country, if they choose, without any restriction ; or remain in it, observing strict neutrality.

With full confidence in the honour and integrity of the inhabitants of the country, I invite the judges, alcaldes, and other civil officers, to retain their offices, and to execute their functions as heretofore, that the public tranquillity may not be disturbed ; at least, until the government of the territory can be more definitely arranged.

All persons holding titles to real estate, or in quiet possession of lands under a colour of right, shall have those titles and rights guarantied to them.

All churches, and the property they contain, in possession of the clergy of California, shall continue in the same rights and possessions they now enjoy.

All provisions and supplies of every kind furnished by the inhabitants for the use of the United States' ships and soldiers will be paid for at fair rates ; and no private property will be taken for public use without just compensation at the moment.

(D)—" General Order," dated " Flag Ship Savannah, July 7, 1846," and signed " John D. Sloat, commander-in-chief of the United States naval forces in the Pacific Ocean."

We are about to land on the territory of Mexico, with whom the United States are at war.   To strike her flag, and to hoist our own in the place of it, is our duty.

It is not only our duty to take California, but to preserve it afterwards as a part of the United States, at all hazards.   To accomplish this, it is of the first importance to cultivate the good opinion of the inhabitants, whom we must reconcile.

I scarcely consider it necessary for me to caution American seamen and marines against the detestable crime of plundering and maltreating unoffending inhabitants.

That no one may misunderstand his duty, the following regulations must be strictly adhered to, as no violation can hope to escape the severest punishment:

1st. On landing, no man is to leave the shore until the commanding officer gives the order to march.

2d. No gun is to be fired, or other act of hostility committed, without express orders from the officer commanding the party.

3d. The officers and boat keepers will keep their respective boats as close to the shore as they will safely float, taking care they do not lay aground, and *remain* in them, prepared to defend themselves against attack; and attentively watch for signals from the ships, as well as from the party on shore.

4th. No man is to quit the ranks or to enter any house for any pretext whatever, without express orders from an officer. · Let every man avoid insult or offence to any unoffending inhabitant, and especially avoid that eternal disgrace which would attach to our names and our country's name by indignity offered to a single female, even let her standing be however low it may.

5th. Plunder of every kind is strictly forbidden. Not only does the plundering of the smallest article from a prize, forfeit all claim to prize money, but the offender must expect to be severely punished.

6th. Finally, let me entreat you, one and all, not to tarnish· our hope of bright success by an act that we shall be ashamed to acknowledge before God and our country.

(E)—Same as (A) with an additional paragraph, as follows:

I hereby invite you to meet me immediately in Monterey, to enter into articles of capitulation, that yourself, officers, and soldiers, with the inhabitants of California, may receive assurances of perfect safety to themselves and property.

(Signed)   **JOHN D. SLOAT,**
Commander-in-chief of the U. S. Naval forces in the Pacific Ocean.
To Señor Don José Castro, *Commandant-general, California.*

(F)—Translation of·the reply of the Commandant-general of the Department of California, under date of " San Juan de Bautista, July 9, 1846," and signed " José Castro :"

The undersigned, Commandant-general of Upper California, has the honour to represent to the· Señor Commander-in-chief of the naval forces· of the United States in the Pacific Ocean, now in ·Monterey, that a band of adventurers, headed by Mr. J. C. Fremont, a captain in the army of the United States, forcibly took possession of the port of Sonoma, hoisting an unknown flag, making prisoners of the chiefs and officers who were there, and committing assassinations and every kind of injury to the lives and property of the inhabitants there. The undersigned is ignorant to what government the invaders of that part of the department belong, and a party of them who are in the neighbourhood of Santa Clara; and as he cannot believe that they belong to the forces commanded by the said Señor Commodore, he will be obliged to him if he will please to make him an explanation on this subject, in order that he may act in conformity with his reply, for neither the undersigned nor a single citizen of the country will permit excess of any kind to be committed by these bands.

(G)—Note to Sr. Don Pio Pico, Angelos, under date " Flag Ship Savannah, Bay of Monterey, July 9, 1846;" and signed "John D. Sloat, Commander-in-chief of the United States naval forces, in the Pacific Ocean, and of the Territory of California."

[First paragraph notices enclosures, and announces the seizure of Monterey.]

I beg your excellency to feel assured that although I come in arms with a powerful force, I come as the best friend of California; and I invite your excellency to meet me at Monterey, that I may satisfy you and the people of California of the fact.

I pledge the word and honour of an American officer, that your excellency will be received with all the respect due to your distinguished situation; and you can depart at any moment you may think proper, and feel every confidence that an American officer expects when his word of honour is pledged.

I have already employed all the means in my power to stop the sacrifice of human life *by the party in the north*, and I trust I shall succeed, provided there is no further opposition.

" The party in the north," alluded to by Captain Sloat, in the closing paragraph of his note to Sr. Pico, of which the preceding is a copy, was the command of Lieutenant-colonel Fremont, who had commenced his belligerent operations in Alta California, on the 7th of March, 1846, and had subsequently carried them on, aided by stragglers and renegades from the United States, and the north of Europe, who had been induced to take up arms, not from any motive of patriotism, but with a desire to drive out and destroy the Mexican settlers, as did the wandering tribes of Israel the Canaanites, that they might possess their herds and their lands ; and for the little service of murder and rapine which these people were *pleased* to perform in furtherance of their own selfish purposes, as well as the designs of the government at Washington, they were *pleased* to demand of the people of the United States only the moderate sum of $50,000 ; [see note from Lieutenant-colonel Fremont, published by Colonel Benton ;] exclusive of the pay of their commander ; and to enable them to abstract thus much of the people's money from the public treasury, General Kearny was directed by General Scott, commander-in-chief of the United States army, to muster them *retrospectively* into the United States service, as volunteers under the act of the 13th of May, 1846, with an understanding that they should be discharged at any time they might signify a wish to that effect. By the payment of these men, the government at Washington adopt the entire of the aggressions commenced in Alta California, by Lieutenant-colonel Fremont, on the 7th of March ; and whatever may have been the private instructions given to him by the Secretary of War, his acts stand confirmed as the acts of the government at Washington.

CHAPTER V.

Captain Stockton's communication to the Government at Washington—His Proclamation to the People of Alta California—His Ordinance—Government, &c.

In the following copy of a communication from Capt. Robert F. Stockton,* who succeeded Captain Sloat in command, to the Secretary of the Navy, will be found a detail of his initiatory step to induct the Mexican people in Alta California into a system of free government, (which, with the paper accompanying the same, were communicated to Congress by the President,) and give to the reader another passage of history :

CUIDAD DE LOS ANGELOS, *August* 28, 1846.

SIR,—You have already been informed of my having, on the 23d of July, assumed the command of the United States forces on the west coast of Mexico. I have now the honour to inform you that the flag of the United States is flying from every commanding position in the territory of California, and that this rich and beautiful country belongs to the United States, and is forever free from Mexican dominion.

On the day after I took this command, I organized the " California battalion of mounted riflemen," by the appointment of all the necessary officers, and received them as volunteers into the service of the United States. Captain Fremont was appointed major, and Lieutenant Gillespie captain of the battalion.

The next day they were embarked on board the sloop-of-war Cyane, Commander Du-

---

* Capt. ROBERT F. STOCKTON is a native of New Jersey, and is a post-captain of some few years' standing. In manners he is pompous; but, nevertheless, is accounted a good officer ; and among the few officers of the navy who are such, he is a politician. During Mr. Tyler's administration he had the command of the U. S. steamer Princeton, and effected the *bad omen* of bursting " *the peace-maker*"—to the destruction of the lives of several eminent citizens.

pont, and sailed from Monterey for San Diego, that they might be landed to the southward of the Mexican forces, amounting to 500 men, under General Castro and Governor Pico, and who were well fortified at the " Camp of the Mesa," three miles from this city.

A few days after the Cyane left, I sailed in the Congress for San Pedro, the port of entry for this department, and thirty miles from this place, where I landed with my gallant sailor army, and marched directly for the redoubtable " Camp of the Mesa."

But when we arrived within twelve miles of the camp, General Castro broke ground and ran for the city of Mexico. The governor of the territory, and the other principal officers, separated in different parties, and ran away in different directions.

Unfortunately, the mounted riflemen did not get up in time to head them off. We have since, however, taken most of the principal officers : the rest will be permitted to remain quiet at home, under the restrictions contained in my proclamation of the 17th.

On the 13th of August, having been joined by Major Fremont with about eighty riflemen, and Mr. Larkin, late American consul, we entered this famous " City of the Angels," the capital of the Californias, and took unmolested possession of the government-house.

Thus, in less than a month after I assumed the command of the United States force in California, we have chased the Mexican army more than three hundred miles along the coast ; pursued them thirty miles in the interior of their own country ; routed and dispersed them, and secured the territory to the United States ; ended the war; restored peace and harmony among the people ; and put a civil government into successful operation.

The Warren and Cyane sailed a few days since to blockade the west coast of Mexico, south of San Diego; and having almost finished my work here, I will sail in the Congress as soon as the store-ship arrives, and I can get supplied with provisions, on a cruise for the protection of our commerce ; and dispose of the other vessels as most effectually to attain that object, and at the same time to keep the southern coast strictly blockaded.

When I leave the territory, I will appoint Major Fremont to be governor, and Lieutenant Gillespie to be secretary.

I enclose you several papers, marked from one to fourteen inclusive, including this letter, and the first number of the " Californian," by which you will see what sort of a government I have established, and how I am proceeding.

I have not time to specify individual merit ; but I cannot omit to say, that I do not think that ardent patriotism and indomitable courage have ever been more evident than amongst the officers and men, 360 in number, from the frigate Congress, who accompanied me on this trying and hazardous march ; a longer march, perhaps, than has ever been made in the interior of a country by sailors, after an enemy. I would likewise say, that the conduct of the officers and men of the whole squadron has been praiseworthy.

I have received your despatch of the 13th of May, and at the same time a Mexican account of the proceedings of Congress, and the President's proclamation, by the United States ship Warren, from Mazatlan.

Faithfully, your obedient servant,
ROBERT F. STOCKTON.

To the Hon. GEORGE BANCROFT,
    Secretary of the Navy, Washington, D. C.

No. 1. [Accompanying document.]—Proclamation of Commodore Stockton, made on the 17th of August, 1846, " to the people of California."

On my approach to this place with the forces under my command, José Castro, the commandant-general of California, buried his artillery and abandoned his fortified camp " of the Mesa," and fled, it is believed, towards Mexico.

With the sailors, the marines, and the California battalion of mounted riflemen, we entered the " City of the Angels," the capital of California, on the 13th of August, and hoisted the North American flag.

The flag of the United States is now flying from every commanding position in the territory, and California is entirely free from Mexican dominion.

The territory of California now belongs to the United States, and will be governed, as soon as circumstances will permit, by officers and laws similar to those by which the other territories of the United States are regulated and protected.

But, until the governor, the secretary, and council are appointed, and the various civil departments of the government are arranged, military law will prevail, and the commander-in-chief will be the governor and protector of the territory.

In the mean time the people will be permitted, and are now requested, to meet in their several towns and departments, at such time and place as they may see fit, to elect civil officers to fill the places of those who decline to continue in office, and to administer the laws according to the former usages of the territory. In all cases where the people fail to elect, the commander-in-chief and governor will make the appointment himself.

All persons, of whatever religion or nation, who faithfully adhere to the new government, will be considered as citizens of the territory, and will be zealously and thoroughly protected in the liberty of conscience, their persons, and property.

No persons will be permitted to remain in the territory who do not agree to support the existing government; and all military men who desire to remain are required to take an oath that they will not take up arms against it, or do or say any thing to disturb its peace.

Nor will any persons, come from where they may, be permitted to settle in the territory, who do not pledge themselves to be, in all respects, obedient to the laws which may be from time to time enacted by the proper authorities of the territory.

All persons who, without special permission, are found with arms outside of their own houses, will be considered as enemies, and will be shipped out of the country.

All thieves will be put to hard labour on the public works, and there kept until compensation is made for the property stolen. ·

The California-battalion of mounted riflemen will be kept in the service of the territory, and constantly on duty, to prevent and punish any aggressions by the Indians, or any other persons, upon the property of individuals, or the peace of the territory; and California shall hereafter be so governed and defended as to give security to the inhabitants, and to defy the power of Mexico.

All persons are required, as long as the territory is under martial law, to be within their houses from ten o'clock at night until sunrise in the morning.

ROBERT F. STOCKTON,

Commander-in-chief and Governor of the Territory of California.

No. 2.—Ordinance of Commodore Stockton.

I, Robert F. Stockton, Commander-in-chief of the United States forces in the Pacific Ocean, and governor of the territory of California, and commander-in-chief of the army of the same, do hereby make known to all men, that having, by right of conquest, taken possession of that territory known by the name of Upper and Lower California, do now declare it to be a territory of the United States, under the name of the territory of California.

And I do, by these presents, further order and decree, that the government of the said territory of California shall be, until altered by the proper authority of the United States, constituted in manner and form as follows; that is to say:

The executive power and authority in and over the said territory shall be vested in a governor, who shall hold his office for four years, unless sooner removed by the President of the United States. The governor shall reside within the said territory; shall be commander-in-chief of the army thereof; shall perform the duties and receive the emoluments of superintendent of Indian affairs, and shall approve of all laws passed by the legislative council before they shall take effect. He may grant pardons for offences against the laws of the said territory, and reprieves for offences against the laws of the United States, until the decision of the President can be made known thereon: he shall commission all officers who shall be appointed to office under the laws of the said territory, and shall take care that the laws be faithfully executed.

There shall be a secretary of the said territory, who shall reside therein and hold his office for four years, unless sooner removed by the President of the United States. He shall record and preserve all the laws and proceedings of the legislative council hereinafter constituted, and all·the acts and proceedings of the governor in his executive department. He shall transmit one copy of the laws and one copy of the executive proceedings, on or before the first·Monday in December in each year, to the President of the United States; and, at the same time, two copies of the laws to the Speaker of the House of Representatives, for the use of Congress. And in case of the death, removal, resignation, or necessary absence of the governor from the territory, the secretary shall have, and he is hereby authorized and required to execute and perform all the powers and duties of the governor during such vacancy or necessary absence.

The legislative power shall be vested in the governor and legislative council. The legis-

c 2

lative council shall consist of seven persons, who shall be appointed by the governor for two years; after which they shall be annually elected by the people.

The power of the legislative council of the territory shall extend to all rightful subjects of legislation; but no law shall be passed interfering with the primary disposal of the soil; no tax shall be imposed upon the property of the United States; nor shall the land or property of non-residents be taxed higher than the lands or other property of residents.

All the laws of the legislative council shall be submitted to, and if disapproved by the governor, the same shall be null and of no effect.

The municipal officers of cities, towns, departments, or districts, heretofore existing in the territory, shall continue to exist, and all their proceedings be regulated and controlled by the laws of Mexico, until otherwise provided for by the governor and legislative council.

All officers of cities, towns, departments, or districts, shall be elected every year by the people, in such manner as may be provided by the governor and legislative council.

The legislative council of the territory of California shall hold its first session at such time and place in said territory as the governor thereof shall appoint and direct; and at said session, or as soon thereafter as may by them be deemed expedient, the said governor and legislative council shall proceed to locate and establish the seat of government for said territory, at such place as they may deem eligible; which place, however, shall thereafter be subject to be changed by the said governor and legislative council, and the time and place of the annual commencement of the session of the said legislative council thereafter shall be on such day and place as the governor and council may appoint.

CHAPTER VI.

Mr. Secretary Bancroft's Communication to Captain Sloat, of the 12th of July, 1846—Do. of the 17th of August—General Scott to General Kearny—Mr. Secretary Mason to Captain Stockton—Stephenson's Expedition—General Kearny's Operations in California, &c.

PREVIOUS to the promulgation of this extraordinary and grand scheme of *"free government"* for the Californians, and its establishment according to the programme of the government at Washington, a communication, of which the following is a copy, passed from the office of the Secretary of the Navy to Captain Sloat:

UNITED STATES NAVY DEPARTMENT, *Washington, July 12, 1846.*

COMMODORE,—Previous instructions have informed you of *the intention of this government, pending the war with Mexico, to take and hold possession of California.* For this end, a company of artillery, with cannon, mortars, and munitions of war, is sent to you in the Lexington, for the purpose of co-operating with you, according to the best of your judgment, and of occupying, under your direction, such post or posts as you may deem expedient, in the Bay of Monterey, or in the Bay of San Francisco, or in both. In the absence of a military officer higher than captain, the selection of the first American post or posts on the waters of the Pacific in California, is left to your discretion.

The object of the United States is, under its rights as a belligerent nation, to possess itself entirely of Upper California.

When San Francisco and Monterey are secured, you will, if possible, send a small vessel of war to take and hold possession of the port of San Diego; and *it would be well to ascertain the views of the inhabitants of Pueblo de los Angelos, who, according to information received here, may be counted upon as desirous of coming under the jurisdiction of the United States.* If you can take possession of it you should do so.

The object of the United States has reference to ultimate peace with Mexico: and if, at that peace, the basis of the uti possidetis *shall be established, the government expects, through your forces, to be found in actual possession of Upper California.*

This will bring with it the necessity of a civil administration. Such a government should be established under your protection; and in selecting persons to hold office, due respect should be had to the wishes of the people of California, as well as to the actual possessors of authority in that province. It may be proper to require an oath of allegiance to the United States from those who are intrusted with authority. You will also assure the people of California of the protection of the United States.

* *In reference to commercial regulations in the ports of which you are in actual possession, ships and produce of the United States should come and go free of duty.*

For your farther instruction, I enclose to you a copy of confidential instructions from the War Department to Brig. Gen. S. W. Kearny, who is ordered overland to California. You will also communicate your instructions to him, and inform him that they have the sanction of the President.

The government relies on the land and naval forces to co-operate with each other in the most friendly and effective manner.

10 *After you shall have secured Upper California,.if your force is sufficient, you .will take possession of, and keep, the harbours on the Gulf of California, as far down, at least, as Guaymas. But this is not to interfere with the permanent occupation of Upper California.*

A regiment of volunteers from the State of New York, to serve during the war, have been called for.by the government, and are expected to sail from the 1st to the 10th of August. This regiment will, in the first instance, report to the naval commander on your station, but will ultimately be under the command of General Kearny, who is appointed to conduct the expedition by land.

The term of three years having nearly expired since you have been in command.of the Pacific squadron, Commodore Shubrick will soon be sent out in the Independence to relieve you. *The department confidently hopes that all Upper California will be in your hands before the relief shall arrive.*   Very respectfully,

GEORGE BANCROFT.

Com. JOHN D. SLOAT, *Commanding U. S. naval forces in the Pacific Ocean.*

It should be understood by the reader, that these communications from the chiefs of the bureaus of the government at Washington, are, in fact, the despatches of the government in Washington, being in the first instance presented to the President in council; and in no case are they sent out unless approved of by him. So that they are the expressions of the will, designs and intentions of the President and his cabinet; and they, consequently, figure the policy of the administration. Understanding the official communications of the heads of the bureaus of the government at Washington in this light, none who read the preceding, from the Secretary of the Navy, will be left to doubt that the conquest of Alta California, with a view to its permanent annexation to the United States, is a design of the President, and a leading measure of his administration. It will be seen by the following communication from the Secretary of the Navy, that the generosity of President Polk will not allow his designs of conquest to extend farther south than Guaymas, which is situated a little south of the 28° of north latitude. Fixing the line of dismemberment there, we should only take a trifle more than a half part of the entire territories of the Republic of Mexico; leaving the other part for another bite—*id est,* "if a treaty of peace shall be made on the basis of the *uti possidetis.*"

NAVY DEPARTMENT, *August* 17, 1846.

COMMODORE,—The United States.being in a state of war by the action of Mexico, it is desired, by the prosecution of hostilities, to hasten the return of peace, and to secure it on advantageous conditions. For .this purpose, orders have been given to the squadron in the Pacific *to take and keep possession of Upper California,* especially of the ports of San Francisco, of Monterey, and of San Diego; and also, if opportunity offer, and the people favour, to take possession, by. an inland .expedition, of Pueblo de los Angelos, near San Diego.

On reaching the Pacific, your first duty will be to ascertain if these orders have been carried into effect. If not, *you will take immediate possession of Upper California,* especially of the three ports of San Francisco, Monterey, and San Diego; *so that, if the treaty of peace shall be made on the basis of the* uti possidetis, *it may leave California to the United States.*

The relations to be maintained with the people of Upper California are to be as friendly as possible. The flag of the United States must be raised, but under it the people are to be allowed as much liberty of self-government as is consistent with the general occupation of the country by the United States. You, as commander-in-chief of the squadron, may exercise the right to interdict the entrance of any vessel or articles that would be unfavourable to our success in the war, into any of the enemy's ports which you may occupy. With this exception, *all United States vessels and merchandise must be allowed by the local authorities of the ports of which you take possession, to come and go free of duty;* but on foreign vessels and goods, reasonable duties may be imposed, collected, and disposed of by the local authorities, under your general superintendence.

A military force has been directed by the Secretary of War to proceed to the western coast of California, for the purpose of co-operation with the navy in taking possession of, and holding, the ports and positions which have been specified, and for otherwise operating against Mexico.

A detachment of these troops, consisting of a company of artillery, under command of Captain Tompkins, has sailed in the United States ship Lexington. A regiment of volunteers, under Colonel Stevenson, will soon sail from New York; and a body of troops, under Brigadier-general Kearny, may reach the coast over Santa Fé. Copies of so much of the instructions to Captain Tompkins and General Kearny as relates to objects requiring co-operation, are herewith enclosed.

By article 6, of the *General Regulations of the Army*, edition of 1825, which is held by the War Department to be still in force, and of which I enclose you a copy, your commission places you, in point of *precedence*, on occasions of ceremony, or, upon meetings for consultation, in the class of major-general; but no officer of the army or navy, whatever may be his rank, can assume any direct command, independent of consent, over an officer of the other service, excepting only when land forces are especially embarked in vessels of war to do the duty of marines.

The President expects and requires, however, the most cordial and effectual co-operation between the officers of the two services, in taking possession of, and holding, the ports and positions of the enemy which are designated in the instructions to either or both branches of the service, and will hold any commander of either branch to a strict responsibility for any failure to preserve harmony and secure the objects proposed.

The land forces which have been, or will be, sent to the Pacific, may be dependent upon the vessels of your squadron for transportation from one point to another, and for shelter and protection in case of being compelled to abandon positions on the coast. It may be necessary also to furnish transportation for their supplies, or to furnish the supplies themselves, by the vessels under your direction.

In all such cases, you will furnish all the assistance in your power, which will not interfere with objects that in your opinion are of greater importance.

You will (taking care, however, to advise with any land officer of high rank—say, of the rank of brigadier-general, who may be at hand) make the necessary regulations for the posts that may be occupied.

Having provided for the full possession of Upper California, the next point of importance is the Gulf of California. From the best judgment I can form, you should take possession of the port of Guaymas. The progress of our arms will probably be such, that, in conjunction with land forces, you will be able to hold possession of Guaymas, and so to reduce all the country north of it on the gulf.

As to the ports south of it, especially Mazatlan and Acapulco, it is not possible to give you special instructions. Generally, you will take possession of, or blockade, according to your best judgment, all Mexican ports, as far as your means allow; but south of Guaymas, if the provinces rise up against the central government, and manifest friendship toward the United States, you may, according to your discretion, enter into a temporary agreement of neutrality. But this must be done only on condition that our ships have free access to their ports, and equal commercial rights with those of other nations; that you are allowed to take in water and fuel; to purchase supplies; to go to and from shore without obstruction, as in time of peace; and that the provinces which are thus neutral shall absolutely abstain from contributing towards the continuance of the war by the central government of Mexico against the United States.

Generally, you will exercise the rights of a belligerent, and bear in mind, that the greater advantages you obtain, the more speedy, and the more advantageous will be the peace.

Should Commodore Biddle be in the Pacific, off the shores of Mexico, at the time you arrive there, you will report yourself to him; and, as long as he remains off the coast of Mexico, you will act under his direction, in concert with him, communicating to him these instructions.

The Savannah, the Warren, and the Levant ought soon to return. If you hear of peace between the United States and Mexico, you will at once send them home.

If war continues, you will send them home singly or in company, at the earliest day they can be spared. The Savannah will go to New York, and the Warren and Levant to Norfolk.

Very respectfully, yours,
GEORGE BANCROFT.

Com. WILLIAM B. SHUBRICK,
Appointed to command the U. S. Naval Forces in the Pacific Ocean.

It is shown by the above communication from the Secretary of the Navy, that permission, or rather instructions were given to the commander of the American naval forces on the Pacific coast of the continent, "to enter into temporary agreements of neutrality" with any of the Mexican provinces, south of Guaymas, who were disposed "to rise up against the central government of Mexico, and to manifest friendship towards the United States." The departments or states of Mexico open to this proposition, are as follows: Sinaloa, Jalisco, Michoacan, Mexico, Puebla, and Oajaca. But the stubborn Mexicans of these states have refused to avail themselves of the liberal offers of their conquering foes.

From the following communication from General Scott to General Kearny, it is to be inferred that Captain Stockton assumed the civil government of Alta California, without the expressed authority, and contrary to the intentions of the government at Washington; and that no authority emanated from General Scott, authorizing any officer of the army formally to declare the annexation of Alta California to the United States:

HEAD-QUARTERS OF THE ARMY, *Washington, November* 3, 1846.

SIR,—We have received from you many official reports—the latest dated September the 16th. A special acknowledgment of them by dates, will go, herewith, from the adjutant-general's office.

Your march upon, and conquest of New Mexico, together with the military dispositions made for holding that province, have won for you, I am authorized to say, the emphatic approbation of the executive, by whom, it is not doubted, your movement upon and occupation of Upper California, will be executed with like energy, judgment, and success.

You will, at Monterey, or the bay at San Francisco, find an engineer officer (Lieutenant Halleck) and a company of the United States artillery, under Captain Tompkins. It is probable that an officer of engineers, or of topographical engineers, has accompanied you from Santa Fé. Those officers, and the company of artillery, aided by other troops under your command, ought promptly to be employed in erecting and garrisoning durable defences for holding the bays of Monterey and San Francisco, together with such other important points in the same province, as you may deem it necessary to occupy. Entrenching tools, ordnance, and ordnance stores went out in the ship Lexington, with Captain Tompkins. Further ordnance supplies may be soon expected.

It is perceived, by despatches received at the Navy Department from the commander of the United States squadron on the coast of the Pacific, that certain volunteers were taken into the service by him, from the settlers about the bays of Monterey and San Francisco, to aid him in seizing and holding that country. With a view to regular payment, it is desirable that those volunteers, if not originally mustered, should be caused by you to be regularly mustered into service (retrospectively) under the volunteer act of May 13, 1846, amended by an act of the following month. This may be done with the distinct understanding that, if not earlier discharged, as no longer needed, you will discharge them at any time they may signify a wish to that effect.

You will probably find certain port charges and regulations established for the harbours of the province, by the commanders of the United States squadron upon its coast. The institution and alteration of such regulations appertain to the naval commander, who is instructed, by the proper department, to confer on the subject, with the commander of the

5

land forces. As established, you will, in your sphere, cause those regulations to be duly respected and enforced. On the other hand, the appointment of temporary collectors at the several ports appertains to the civil governor of the province, who will be, for the time, the senior officer of the land forces in the country. Collectors, however, who have been already appointed by the naval commander, will not be unnecessarily changed.

As a guide to the civil governor of Upper California, in our hands, see the letter of June the 3d (last) addressed to you by the Secretary of War. You will not, however, formally declare the province to be annexed. Permanent incorporation of the territory must depend on the government of the United States.

After occupying, with our forces, all necessary points in Upper California, and establishing a temporary civil government therein, as well as assuring yourself of its internal tranquillity, and the absence of any danger of reconquest on the part of Mexico, you may charge Colonel Mason, United States first dragoons, the bearer of this open letter, or land officer next in rank to your own, with your several duties, and return yourself, with a sufficient escort of troops, to St. Louis, Missouri. But the body of the United States dragoons that accompanied you to California will remain there until further orders.

It is not known what portion of the Missouri volunteers, if any, marched with you from Santa Fé to the Pacific. If any, it is necessary to provide for their return to their homes and honourable discharge; and, on the same supposition, they may serve you as a sufficient escort to Missouri.

It is known that Lieutenant-colonel Fremont, of the United States rifle regiment, was, in July last, with a party of men ·in the service of the United States topographical engineers, in the neighbourhood of San Francisco, or Monterey bay, engaged in joint operations against Mexico with the United States squadron on that coast. Should you find him there, it is desired that you do not detain him, against his wishes, a moment longer than the necessities of the service may require.

I need scarcely enjoin deference and the utmost cordiality on the part of our land forces towards those of our navy in the joint service on the distant coast of California. Reciprocity may be cordially expected; and towards that end, frequent conferences between commanders of the two arms are recommended. Harmony in co-operation, and success cannot but follow.

Measures have been taken to supply the disbursing officers who have preceded, and who may accompany you, with all necessary funds. Of those measures you will be informed by Colonel Mason.

I remain, sir, with great respect, your obedient servant,
WINFIELD SCOTT.

· To Brig. Gen. STEPHEN W. KEARNY,
U. S. A. Commanding U. S. forces 10th Military Dept.

By the preceding communication it will be perceived, that General Scott, on the 3d of November, 1846, an entire month before the Secretary of War made his annual report, had full knowledge of the true character of the men serving under Lieutenant-colonel Fremont, of whom he says—" It is KNOWN that Lieutenant-colonel Fremont, of the United States rifle regiment, was in July last, with a party of men in the service of the United States topographical engineers, in the neighbourhood of San Francisco, or Monterey bay, engaged in joint operations against Mexico with the United States squadron on the coast :" and yet the Secretary of War assures the American people, in his report, that " not an officer or soldier of the United States army accompanied him." In common parlance—in fact—and for all practical purposes, do not men who are " in the service of the United States topographical engineers," belong to the United States army; as much so as the California rifle battalion, or any company of Texas rangers, who have followed the trail of " old Rough and Ready !" It is just to note the assertion in the following communication, that—" The existing war with Mexico has been commenced by her." Such is the declaration of Mr. Mason, an adviser and supporter of ex-president John Tyler, who has spread his sails, and now follows in the wake of James K. Polk, William L. Marcy, and Mr. Ritchie, as the successor of George Bancroft. The facts are submitted to the reader:

[*Confidential.*]

UNITED STATES NAVY DEPARTMENT, *Washington, Nov. 5, 1846.*

COMMODORE,—Commodore Sloat has arrived in this city, and delivered your letter of the 28th July ult., with the copy of your address to the people of California, which accompanied it. The department is gratified that you joined the squadron before the state of the commodore's health rendered it necessary for him to relinquish his important command.

The difficulties and embarrassments of the command, without a knowledge of the proceedings of Congress on the subject of the war with Mexico, and in the absence of the instructions of the department, which followed these proceedings, are justly appreciated; and it is highly gratifying that so much has been done in anticipation of the orders which have been transmitted.

You will, without doubt, have received the despatches of the 15th of May last, addressed to Commodore Sloat; and I now send you, for your guidance, a copy of instructions to Commodore Shubrick of the 17th August. He sailed early in September, in the razee Independence, with orders to join the squadron with the least possible delay. On his assuming the command, you may hoist a red pennant. If you prefer, you may hoist your pennant on the Savannah, and return home with her and the Warren.

The existing war with Mexico has been ·commenced by her. Every disposition was felt and manifested by the United States government to procure redress for the injuries of which we complained, and to settle all complaints on her part, in the spirit of peace and of justice which has ever characterized our intercourse with foreign nations. That disposition still exists ; and whenever the authorities of Mexico shall manifest a willingness to adjust unsettled points of controversy between the two republics, and to restore an honourable peace, they will be met in a corresponding spirit.

This consummation is not to be expected, nor is our national honour to be maintained, without a vigorous prosecution of the war on our part. Without being animated by any ambitious spirit of conquest, our naval and military forces must hold the ports and territory of the enemy, of which possession has been obtained by their arms. You will, therefore, under no circumstances, voluntarily lower the flag of the United States, or relinquish the actual possession of Upper California. Of other points of the Mexican territory, which the forces under your command may occupy, you will maintain the possession, or withdraw, as in your judgment may be most advantageous in the prosecution of the war.

In regard to your intercourse with the inhabitants of the country, your views are judicious, and you will conform to the instructions heretofore given. You will exercise the rights of a belligerent ; and if you find that the liberal policy of our government, in purchasing and paying for required supplies, is misunderstood, and its exercise is injurious to the public interest, you are at liberty to take them from the enemy without compensation, or pay such prices as may be deemed just and reasonable. The best policy in this respect depends on a knowledge of circumstances in which you are placed, and is left to your discretion.

The Secretary of War has ordered Col. R. B. Mason, 1st United States dragoons, to proceed to California, via Panama, who will command the troops and conduct the military operations in the Mexican territory bordering on the Pacific, in the absence of Brigadier-general Kearny. The commander of the naval forces will consult and co-operate with him in his command to the same extent as if he held a higher rank in the army. In all questions of relative rank, he is to be regarded as having only the rank of colonel.

The President has deemed it best for the public interests to invest the military officer commanding with the direction of the operations on land, and with the administrative functions of government over the people and territory occupied by us. You will relinquish to Colonel Mason, or to General Kearny, if the latter shall arrive before you have done so, the entire control over these matters, and turn over to him all papers necessary to the performance of his duties. ·If officers of the navy are employed in the performance of civil or military duties, you will withdraw or continue them, at your discretion, taking care to put them to their appropriate duty in the squadron, if the army officer, commanding does not wish their services on land.

The establishment of port regulations is a subject over which it is deemed by the President most appropriate that the·naval commander shall exercise jurisdiction. You will establish these, and communicate them to the military commander, who will carry them into effect so far as his co-operation may be necessary, suggesting for your consideration modifications or alterations.

The regulation of the import trade is also confided to you. The conditions under which vessels of our own citizens and of neutrals may be admitted into ports of the enemy in your possession, will be prescribed by you, subject to the instructions heretofore given. To aid you, copies of instructions to the collectors in the United States, from the Treasury Department, on the same subject, are enclosed. On cargoes of neutrals imported into such ports, you may impose moderate duties, not greater in amount than those collected in the ports of the United States. The collection of these duties will be made by civil officers, to be appointed, and subject to the same rules as other persons charged with civil duties in the country. These appointments will be made by the military officers in consultation with you.

The President directs me to impress most earnestly on the naval officers, as it is impressed on those of the army, the importance of harmony in the performance of their delicate duties, while co-operating. They are arms of one body, and will, I doubt not, vie with each other in showing which can render the most efficient aid to the other in the execution of common orders, and in sustaining the national honour, which is confided to both.

You will make your communications to the department as frequent as possible.

The great distance at which your command is placed, and the impossibility of maintaining a frequent or regular communication with you, necessarily induce the department to leave much of the details of your operations to your discretion. The confident belief is entertained, that, with the general outline given in the instructions, you will pursue a course which will make the enemy sensible of our power to inflict on them the evils of war, while it will secure to the United States, if a definitive treaty of peace shall give us California, a population impressed with our justice, grateful for our clemency, and prepared to love our institutions and to honour our flag.

On your being relieved in the command of the squadron, you will hand your instructions to the officer relieving you.

I am, very respectfully, your obedient servant,   JOHN Y. MASON.

Com. ROBERT F. STOCKTON, *Comm'ng U. S. naval forces on the west coast of Mexico.*

The Secretary of the Navy informs Captain Stockton that " the President has deemed it best for the public interest to invest the military officer commanding with the direction of the operations on land, and with the administrative functions of government over the people and territory occupied by us ;" and further suggests that " the Secretary of War has ordered Col. R. B. Mason, of the 1st regiment U. S. dragoons, to proceed to California, via Panama, who will command the troops and conduct the military operations in the Mexican territory bordering on the Pacific, in the absence of Brigadier-general Kearny."*

General Kearny had been assigned to the command of the troops in California, and promoted from the rank of colonel to that of brigadier-general, with the express view to give him rank corresponding with his command. But after the occupation of Santa Fé, and as he was about to enter upon his line of march for California, General Kearny, under date of " Santa Fé, September 16, 1846," addressed the adjutant-general as follows :—" I have now respectfully to ask that, in the event of our getting possession of Upper California—of establishing a civil government there—securing peace, quiet, and order, among the inhabitants, and precluding the possibility of the Mexicans again having control there, I may be permitted to leave there next summer with the 1st dragoons, and march them back to Fort Leavenworth, on the Missouri." This request from General Kearny was acceded to by the Secretary of War, as it had been intended by him to invest one Jonathan D. Stevenson,† of the city of New York, with the civil government of Cali-

---

* Brig. Gen. STEPHEN W. KEARNY commenced his career (as the writer is informed) as an officer in the U. S. army, during the last war with Great Britain. Whether he has been continuously in the service since he entered it, is not now recollected. Upon the creation of the 1st regiment of U. S. dragoons, in 1835, he was appointed one of the field-officers of that regiment; and at the commencement of the war with Mexico he was colonel-in-chief.

† JONATHAN D. STEVENSON is a native of the city of New York, and is now about fifty

·fornia; and, with this view, the Secretary of War commissioned Stevenson to raise a regiment of volunteers for service in California. But Stevenson's notoriously bad character, with a still worse course of conduct, pursued during the time he was engaged in the organization of his regiment in New York, compelled the Secretary of War to change his intentions with regard to the investment of Stevenson with the civil government of California, and to assign Colonel Mason, of the 1st regiment United States dragoons, to duty in California, and to act as ·military commandant and civil governor, when-ever it should please General Kearny to retire from the post.

The following copies of communications received by the government at Washington, from General Kearny, embrace full accounts of his operations in California, and may be .accepted, as forming only a single page in the history of what the President. denominated, in his last annual message, " the bloodless acquisition of the possession of the Californias !"

'' HEAD-QUARTERS, ARMY OF THE WEST,
 ı San Diego, Upper California, Dec. 12, 1846.

SIR,—As I have previously reported to you, I left Santa Fé (New Mexico) for this country, on the 25th of September, with 300 of the 1st dragoons, under Major Sumner. We crossed to the banks of the Del Norte at Albuquerque, (sixty-five miles below Santa Fé,) continued down on that bank till the 6th of October, when we met Mr. Kit Carson, with a party of sixteen men, on his way to Washington city, with a mail and papers—an express from Commodore Stockton and Lieutenant-colonel Fremont, reporting that the Califor-nias were already in possession of the Americans under their command; that the Ameri-can flag was flying from every important position in the territory, and that the country was forever free from Mexican control; the war ended, and peace and harmony established among the people. In consequence of this information, I directed that 200 dragoons under Major Sumner should remain in New Mexico, and that the other 100, with two mounted howitzers, under Captain Moore, should accompany me, as a guard, to Upper California. With this guard, we continued our march to the south, on the right bank of the Del Norte, to the distance of about 230 miles below Santa Fé, when, leaving that river on the 15th of October, in about the thirty-third degree of latitude, we marched westward for the copper mines, which we reached on the 18th, and on the 20th reached the river Gila; proceeded down the Gila, crossing, and recrossing it as often as obstructions in our front rendered it necessary; on the 11th of November, reached the Pimos village, about eighty miles from the settlements in Sonora. These Indians we found honest, and living comfortably, having made a good crop this year; and we remained with them two days to rest our men, and recruit our animals, and obtain provisions. On the 22d of November, reached the mouth of the Gila, in latitude about thirty-two degrees—our whole march on this river having been nearly 500 miles, and with but very little exception, between the thirty-second and thirty-third parallels of latitude.

This river, (the Gila,) more particularly the northern side, is bounded nearly the whole distance by a range of lofty mountains; and if a tolerable wagon road to its mouth, from the Del Norte, is ever discovered, it must be on the south side. The country is destitute of timber, producing but few cotton-wood and mosquite trees; and though the soil on the bottom lands is generally good, yet we found but very little grass or vegetation, in conse-quence of the dryness of the climate and the little rain which falls here. The Pimos Indians, who make good crops of wheat, corn, vegetables, &c., irrigate the land by water from the Gila, as did the Aztecs, (the. former inhabitants of the country,) the remains of

---

years of age. His parents were English; his father having served many years in the British navy as a common sailor. In New York he followed the business of a boatman. Jonathan was bred to the business of a tailor; but, for a short servitude, he was in the em-ployment of the late ex-Governor Tompkins, as a hired man for all work. After leaving Governor Tompkins's employment, he set up a tailor's shop in Canal street; and from thence he removed to Water street; and afterwards changed his business to keeping an eat-ing and drinking house. He possesses neither military skill nor experience; and couse-quently, his selection, by the Secretary of War, to command a regiment of volunteers in California, struck the citizens of New York, generally, with surprise.

D

whose suquias, or little canals, were seen by us, as well as the position of many of their dwellings, and a large quantity of broken pottery and earthenware used by them.

We crossed the Colorado about ten miles below the mouth of the Gila, and, marching near it about thirty miles further, turned off and crossed the desert—a distance of about sixty miles—without water or grass.

On the 2d of December, reached Warner's rancho, (Agua Caliente,) the frontier settlement in California, on the route leading to Sonora. On the 4th, marched to Mr. Stokes's rancho, (San Isabella,) and on the 5th, were met by a small party of volunteers, under Captain Gillespie, sent out from San Diego, by Commodore Stockton, to give us what information they possessed of the enemy, 600 or 700 of whom are now said to be in arms and in the field throughout the territory, determined upon opposing the Americans and resisting their authority in the country. Encamped that night near another rancho (San Maria) of Mr. Stokes, about forty miles from San Diego.

The journals and maps, kept and prepared by Captain Johnston, (my aid-de-camp,) and those by Lieutenant Emory, topographical engineers, which will accompany or follow this report, will render any thing further from me on this subject unnecessary.

Very respectfully, your obedient servant,
STEPHEN W. KEARNY, Brig. Gen. U. S. A.
Brig. Gen. Roger Jones, Adj't Gen. U. S. A.

HEAD-QUARTERS, ARMY OF THE WEST,
San Diego, Upper California, Dec. 13, 1846.
Sir,—In my communication to you, of yesterday's date, I brought the reports of the movements of my guard up to the morning of the 5th instant, in a camp near a rancho of Mr. Stokes, (Santa Maria,) about forty miles from San Diego.

Having learned from Captain Gillespie, of the volunteers, that there was an armed party of Californians, with a number of extra horses, at San Pasqual, three leagues distant, on a road leading to this place, I sent Lieutenant Hammond, 1st dragoons, with a few men to make a reconnoissance of them. He returned at two in the morning of the 6th instant, reporting that he had found the party in the place mentioned, and that he had been seen. though not pursued by them. I then determined that I would march for and attack them by break of day. Arrangements were accordingly made for the purpose. My aid-de-camp, Captain Johnston, dragoons, was assigned to the command of the advanced guard of twelve dragoons, mounted on the best horses we had; then followed about fifty dragoons under Captain Moore, mounted, with but few exceptions, on the tired mules they had ridden from Santa Fé, (New Mexico, 1050 miles,) then about twenty volunteers of Captain Gibson's company under his command, and that of Captain Gillespie; then followed our two mountain howitzers, with dragoons to manage them, and under the charge of Lieutenant Davidson, of the regiment. The remainder of the dragoons, volunteers, and citizens, employed by the officers of the staff, &c., were placed under the command of Major Swords, (quartermaster,) with orders to follow on our trail with the baggage, and to see to its safety.

As the day (December 6) dawned, we approached the enemy at San Pasqual, who was already in the saddle, when Captain Johnston made a furious charge upon them with his advanced guard, and was in a short time after supported by the dragoons; soon after which the enemy gave way, having kept up, from the beginning, a continued fire upon us. Upon the retreat of the enemy, Captain Moore led off rapidly in pursuit, accompanied by the dragoons, mounted on horses, and was followed, though slowly, by the others on their tired mules; the enemy, well mounted, and among them the best horsemen in the world, after retreating about half a mile, and seeing an interval between Captain Moore with his advance, and the dragoons coming to his support, rallied their whole force, charged with their lances, and on account of their greatly superior numbers, but few of us in front remained untouched; for five minutes they held the ground from us, when our men coming up, we again drove them, and they fled from the field not to return to it, which we occupied and encamped upon.

A most melancholy duty now remains for me; it is to report the death of my aid-de-camp, Captain Johnston, who was shot dead at the commencement of the action; of Captain Moore, who was lanced just previous to the final retreat of the enemy, and of Lieutenant Hammond, also lanced, and who survived but a few hours. We had also killed two sergeants, two corporals, and ten privates of the 1st dragoons; one private of the volunteers, and one man, an engagee in the topographical department. Among the wounded are myself, (in two places,) Lieutenant Warner, topographical engineers, (in three places,) Captains Gillespie and Gibson, of the volunteers, (the former in three places,) one serjeant, one bugle-man and nine privates of the dragoons; many of these surviving from two to ten lance-wounds, most of them when unhorsed and incapable of resistance.

Our howitzers were not brought into action; but coming to the front, at the close of it, before they were turned, so as to admit of being fired upon by the retreating enemy, the two mules before one of them got alarmed, and freeing themselves from their drivers, ran off and among the enemy, and were thus lost to us.

The enemy proved to be a party of about 160 Californians, under Andreas Pico, brother of the late governor; the number of their dead and wounded must have been considerable, though I have no means of ascertaining how many, as, just previous to their final retreat, they carried off all excepting six.

The great number of our killed and wounded proves that our officers and men have fully sustained the high character and reputation of our troops; and the victory thus gained over more than double our force, may assist in forming the wreath of our national glory.

I have to return my thanks to many for their gallantry and good conduct on the field, and particularly to Captain Turner, 1st dragoons, (assistant acting adjutant-general,) and to Lieutenant Emory, topographical engineers, who were active in the performance of their duties, and in conveying orders from me to the command.

On the morning of the 7th, having made ambulances for our wounded, and interred the dead, we proceeded on our march, when the enemy showed himself, occupying the hills in our front, but which they left as we approached; till, reaching San Bernado, a party of them took possession of a hill near to it, and maintained their position until attacked by our advance who quickly drove them from it, killing and wounding five of their number, with no loss on our part.

On account of our wounded men, and upon the report of the surgeon that rest was necessary for them, we remained at this place till the morning of the 11th, when Lieutenant Gray, of the navy, in command of a party of sailors and marines, sent out from San Diego by Commodore Stockton, joined us. We proceeded at ten a. m., the enemy no longer showing himself; and on the 12th (yesterday) we reached this place; and I have now to offer my thanks to Commodore Stockton, and all of his gallant command, for the very many kind attentions we have received and continue to receive from them.

Very respectfully, your obedient servant,
STEPHEN W. KEARNY, *Brig. Gen. U. S. A.*
Brig. Gen. ROGER JONES, *Adjutant-General, U. S. A.*

HEAD-QUARTERS, ARMY OF THE WEST,
Cuidad de los Angelos, Upper California, January 12, 1847.

SIR,—I have the honour to report that at the request of Com. Robert F. Stockton, United States navy, (who, in September last, assumed the title of Governor of California,) I consented to take command of an expedition to this place, (the capital of the country,) and that, on the 29th of December, I left San Diego with about 500 men, consisting of sixty dismounted dragoons under Captain Turner, fifty California volunteers, and the remainder of marines and sailors, with a battery of artillery—Lieutenant Emory (topographical engineer) acting as assistant adjutant-general. Commodore Stockton accompanied us.

We proceeded on our route without seeing the enemy, till on the 8th instant, when they showed themselves in full force of 600 mounted men, with four pieces of artillery, under their governor, (Flores,) occupying the heights in front of us, which commanded the crossing of the river San Gabriel, and they ready to oppose our further progress. The necessary disposition of our troops was immediately made, by covering our front with a strong party of skirmishers, placing our wagons and baggage train in rear of them, and protecting the flanks and rear with the remainder of the command. We then proceeded, forded the river, carried the heights, and drove the enemy from them after an action of about an hour and a half, during which they made a charge upon our left flank, which was repulsed; soon after which they retreated and left us in possession of the field, on which we encamped that night.

The next day (the 9th instant) we proceeded on our march at the usual hour, the enemy in our front and on our flanks; and when we reached the plains of the Mesa, their artillery again opened upon us, when their fire was returned by our guns as we advanced; and after hovering around and near us for about two hours, occasionally skirmishing with us during that time, they concentrated their force and made another charge on our left flank, which was quickly repulsed; shortly after which they retired, we continuing our march, and we (in the afternoon) encamped on the banks of the Mesa, three miles below this city, which we entered the following morning (the 10th instant) without further molestation.

Our loss in the actions of the 8th and 9th was small, being but one private killed, and two officers (Lieutenant Rowan, of the navy, and Captain Gillespie of the volunteers) and eleven privates wounded. The enemy, mounted on fine horses, and being the best riders in the world, carried off their killed and wounded, and we know not the number of them, though it must have been considerable.

Very respectfully, your obedient servant,

STEPHEN W. KEARNY, *Brig. Gen. U. S. A.*

Brig. Gen. ROGER JONES, *Adjutant-general, U. S. A.*

Statement of killed and wounded in the action of the 8th of January, 1847.

Killed.—Frederic Strauss, seaman, United States ship Portsmouth, artillery corps: cannon-shot in the neck.

Wounded.—1st, Jacob Hait, volunteer, artillery driver, wound in left breast; died on evening of 9th. 2d, Thos. Smith, ordinary seaman, United States ship Cyane, company D, musketeers, shot by accident through the right thigh; died on the 9th. 3d, William Cope, seaman, United States ship Savannah, company B, musketeers, wound in the right thigh and right arm; severe. 4th, George Bantum, ordinary seaman, United States ship Cyane, pikeman, punctured wound of hand, accidental; slight. 5th, Patrick Campbell, seaman, United States ship Cyane, company D, musketeers, wound in thigh by spent ball: slight. 6th, William Scott, private, United States marine corps, ship Portsmouth, wound in the chest, spent ball; slight. 7th, James Hendry, seaman, United States ship Congress, company A, musketeers, spent ball, wound over stomach; slight. 8th, Joseph Wilson, seaman, United States ship Congress, company A, musketeers, wound in right thigh, spent ball; slight. 9th, Ivory Coffin, seaman, United States ship Savannah, company B, musketeers, contusion of right knee, spent ball; slight.

Wounded on the 9th.—1st, Mark A. Child, private, company C, 1st regiment United States dragoons, gunshot wound in right heel, penetrating upwards into the ankle joint; severe. 2d, John Campbell, ordinary seaman, United States ship Congress, company D, carbineers, wound in right foot, second toe amputated; accidental discharge of his own carbine. 3d, Geo. Crawford, boatswain's mate, United States ship Cyane, company D, musketeers, wound in left thigh; severe. Lieutenant Rowan, United States navy, and Captain Gillespie, California battalion, volunteers, contused slightly by spent balls.

I am, sir, most respectfully, your obedient servant,

JOHN S. GRIFFIN, *Assistant Surgeon, U. S. N.*

Captain WILLIAM H. EMORY, *Assistant Adjutant-general, U. S. Forces.*

Cuidad de los Angelos, California, January 11, 1847.

HEAD-QUARTERS, ARMY OF THE WEST,
Cuidad de los Angelos, January 14th, 1847.

SIR,—This morning, Lieutenant-colonel Fremont, of the regiment of mounted riflemen, reached here with 400 volunteers from the Sacramento; the enemy capitulated with him yesterday, near San Fernando, agreeing to lay down their arms, and we have now the prospect of having peace and quietness in the country, which I hope may not be interrupted again.

I have not yet received any information of the troops which were to come from New York, nor of those to follow me from New Mexico, but presume they will be here before long. On their arrival, I shall, agreeably to the instructions of the President of the United States, have the management of affairs in this country, and will endeavour to carry out his views in relation to it.

Very respectfully, your obedient servant,

STEPHEN W. KEARNY, *Brig. Gen. U. S. A.*

Brig. Gen. ROGER JONES, *Adjutant-general, U. S. A.*

CHAPTER VII.

Differences between General Kearny and Captain Stockton—Captain Stockton's Report— Lieutenant-colonel Fremont's Treaty—Letter of late U. S. Consul—Lieutenant Talbot's Letter—Lieutenant-colonel Fremont's Explanation—Letter from Mr. Secretary Marcy to General Kearny, &c.

To the communications contained in the preceding chapter, from General Kearny, the following additional ones, (copies of which were furnished for publication from the Navy Department at Washington,) from Captain Stockton, are added, as constituting a more perfect account of the military operations in California.

General Kearny acknowledges the presence of Captain Stockton; and states—That "at the request of *Commodore* R. F. Stockton, U. S. Navy, who in September last had *assumed* the title of *Governor of California*, I consented to take command of an expedition to this place, [Cuidad de los Angelos,] and, on the 29th of December, I left San Diego with 500 men, consisting of about sixty dismounted dragoons under Captain Turner, fifty California volunteers, and the remainder of marines and sailors, with a battery of artillery." The same movement is thus described by Captain Stockton :—" We left San Diego on the 29th of December, with about 600 fighting men, composed of detachments from the ships Congress, Savannah, Portsmouth and Cyane, aided by General Kearny with a detachment of sixty men on foot, from the 1st regiment U. S. dragoons, and by Captain Gillespie with sixty mounted riflemen." The preceding is the only mention made by Captain Stockton of the presence and services of General Kearny, and in this it will be seen that Captain Stockton, instead of acknowledging General Kearny as being in command, mentions him only as the leader of sixty dismounted dragoons, and puts his services on a par with those of Captain Gillespie, the commander of a company of mounted volunteers. There could exist no good feeling between commanders who could authorize such reports of the performance of their public duties : and they look bad in history.

HEAD-QUARTERS, *Cuidad de los Angelos, January* 11, 1847.

SIR,—I have the honour to inform you that it has pleased God to crown our poor efforts to put down the rebellion, and to retrieve the credit of our arms, with the most complete success. The insurgents determined, with their whole force, to meet us on our march from San Diego to this place, and to decide the fate of the territory by a general battle.

Having made the best preparation I could, in the face of a boasting and vigilant enemy, we left San Diego on the 29th day of December, (that portion of the insurgent army who had been watching and annoying us, having left to join the main body,) with about 600 fighting men, composed of detachments from the ships Congress, Savannah, Portsmouth, and Cyane, aided by General Kearny, with a detachment of sixty men on foot, from the 1st regiment of United States dragoons, and by Captain Gillespie, with sixty mounted riflemen.

We marched nearly one hundred and forty miles in ten days, and found the rebels on the 8th day of January in a strong position, on the high bank of the Rio San Gabriel, with 600 mounted men and four pieces of artillery, prepared to dispute our passage across the river.

We waded through the water, dragging our guns after us against the galling fire of the enemy, without exchanging a shot until we reached the opposite shore ; when the fight became general, and our troops having repelled a charge of the enemy, charged up the bank in most gallant manner, and gained a complete victory over the insurgent army.

The next day, on our march across the plains of the "Mesa" to this place, the insurgents made another desperate effort to save the capital and their own necks ; they were

6   D 2

concealed with their artillery in a ravine until we came within gunshot, when they opened a brisk fire from their field-pieces on our right flank, and at the same time charged both on our front and rear. We soon silenced their guns, and repelled the charge, when they fled, and permitted us the next morning to march into town without any further opposition.

We have rescued the country from the hands of the insurgents, but I fear that the absence of Col. Fremont's battalion of mounted riflemen will enable most of the Mexican officers, who have broken their parole, to escape to Sonora.

I am happy to say that our loss in killed and wounded does not exceed twenty, whilst we are informed that the enemy has lost between seventy and eighty.

This despatch must go immediately; I will wait another opportunity to furnish you with the details of these two battles, and the gallant conduct of the officers and men under my command, with their names. Faithfully, your obedient servant,

R. F. STOCKTON, *Commodore, &c.*

To the Hon. GEORGE BANCROFT, *Secretary of the Navy, Washington, D. C.*

P. S. Enclosed I have the honour to send to you a translation of the letter handed to me by the commissioners mentioned in another part of this despatch, sent by José Ma. Flores, to negotiate a peace honourable to both nations. The verbal answer, stated in another page of this letter, was sent to this renowned general and commander-in-chief. He had violated his honour, and I would not treat with him nor write to him.

HEAD-QUARTERS, *Cuidad de los Angelos, January* 15, 1847.

SIR,—Referring to my letter of the 11th, I have the honour to inform you of the arrival of Lieutenant-colonel Fremont at this place, with 400 men—that some of the insurgents have made their escape to Sonora, and that the rest have surrendered to our arms.

Immediately after the battles of the 8th and 9th, they began to disperse; and I am sorry to say that their leader, José Ma. Flores, made his escape, and that the others have been pardoned by a capitulation agreed upon by Lieutenant-colonel Fremont.

José Ma. Flores, the commander of the insurgent forces, two or three days previous to the 8th, sent two commissioners with a flag of truce to my camp, to make "a treaty of peace." I informed the commissioners that I could not recognise José Ma. Flores, who had broken his parole, as an honourable man, or as one having any rightful authority, or worthy to be treated with—that he was a rebel in arms, and if I caught him I would have him shot. It seems that not being able to negotiate with me, and having lost the battles of the 8th and 9th, they met Colonel Fremont on the 12th instant, on his way here, who, not knowing what had occurred, entered into the capitulation with them, which I now send to you; and, although I refused to do it myself, still I have thought it best to approve it.

The territory of California is again tranquil, and the civil government formed by me is again in operation in the places where it was interrupted by the insurgents.

Colonel Fremont has 500 men in his battalion, which will be quite sufficient to preserve the peace of the territory; and I will immediately withdraw my sailors and marines, and sail as soon as possible for the coast of Mexico, where I hope they will give a good account of themselves. Faithfully, your obedient servant,

R. F. STOCKTON, *Commodore, &c.*

To the Hon. GEORGE BANCROFT, *Secretary of the Navy, Washington, D. C.*

To all whom these presents shall come, greeting:

Know ye that, in consequence of propositions of peace, or cessation of hostilities being submitted to me as commandant of the California battalion of United States forces, which has so far been acceded to by me, as to cause me to appoint a board of commissioners to confer with a similar board appointed by the Californians; and it requiring a little time to close the negotiations, it is agreed upon and ordered by me, that an entire cessation of hostilities shall take place until to-morrow afternoon, (January 13th,) and that the said Californians be permitted to bring in their wounded to the mission of San Fernandez, where also, if they choose, they can remove their camp, to facilitate said negotiations.

Given under my hand and seal, this 12th day of January, 1847.

JOHN C. FREMONT,

Lieutenant-colonel U. S. A., and Military Commandant of California.

Articles of capitulation made and entered into at the rancho of Cowanga, this thirteenth day of January, Anno Domini, eighteen hundred and forty-seven, between P. B. Reading, major, Louis McLane, jr., commanding artillery, William H. Russell, ordnance officer, commissioners appointed by John C. Fremont, Lieutenant-colonel, United States army, and military commandant of the territory of California, and José Antonio Carillo, commandant Escuadron, Augustine Olvera, deputado, commissioners appointed by Don Andres Pico, commander-in-chief of the Californian forces under the Mexican flag :—

ARTICLE 1. The commissioners on the part of the Californians agree that their entire force shall, on presentation of themselves to Lieutenant-colonel.Fremont, deliver up their artillery and public arms, and that they shall return peaceably to their homes, conforming to the laws and regulations of the United States, and not again take up arms during the war between the United States and Mexico, but will assist and aid in placing the country in a state of peace and tranquillity.

ARTICLE 2. The commissioners on the part of Lieutenant-colonel Fremont, agree and bind themselves, on the fulfilment of the first article by the Californians, that they shall be guarantied protection of life and property, whether on parole or otherwise.

ARTICLE 3. That until a treaty of peace be made and signed between the United States of North America and the Republic of Mexico, no Californian or other Mexican citizen shall be bound to take the oath of allegiance.

ARTICLE 4. That any Californian or other citizen of Mexico desiring, is permitted by this capitulation to leave the country without let or hindrance.

ARTICLE 5. That in virtue of the aforesaid articles, equal rights and privileges are vouchsafed to every citizen of California as are enjoyed by the citizens of the United States of North America.

ARTICLE 6. All officers, citizens, foreigners, or others, shall receive the protection guarantied by the 2d article.

ARTICLE 7. This capitulation is intended to be no bar in effecting such arrangements as may in future be in justice required by both parties.

P. B. READING, *Major California Battalion.*
WM. H. RUSSELL, *Ord. officer of California Bat.*
LOUIS McLANE, Jr., *Command'g Art., California Bat.*
JOSÉ ANTO. CARILLO, *Commandante de Escuadron.*
AUGUSTINE OLVERA, *Deputado.*
Approved :   JOHN C. FREMONT,
Lt. Col. U. S. A. and Military Commander of California.
Approbado :   '   ANDRES PICO,
Com. de Escuadron en gefe de las'fuerzas nacionales en California.

ADDITIONAL ARTICLE.

That the paroles of all officers, citizens, and others of the United States, and of naturalized citizens of Mexico, are by this foregoing capitulation cancelled, and every condition of said paroles from and after this date, are of no farther force and effect, and all prisoners of both parties are hereby released.

Cuidad de los Angelos, Jan. 16, 1847.

P. B. READING, *Major California Battalion.*   ·
WM. H. RUSSELL, *Ord. officer of California Bat.*
LOUIS McLANE, Jr., *Command'g Art., California Bat.*
JOSÉ ANTO. CARILLO, *Commandante de Escuadron.*
AUGUSTINE OLVERA, *Deputado.*
Approved :   JOHN C. FREMONT,
Lt. Col. U. S. A., and Military Commander of California.
Approbado :   ANDRES PICO,
Com. de Escuadron en gefe de las fuerzas nacionales en Californias.

[TRANSLATION.]

Civil and military government of the Department of California.   ·.   ·

The undersigned, governor and commandant-general of the department and commander-in-chief of the national troops, has the honour to address himself to the commander-in-chief of the naval and land forces of the United States of North America, to say that he has been informed by persons worthy of credit, that it is probable at this time the differences which have altered the relations of friendship between the Mexican republic and that of the United States of North America have ceased, and that you looked for the news of the arrangement between the two governments by the schooner Shark, expected every moment on this coast.   .   . .

A number of days have elapsed since the undersigned was invited by several foreign gentlemen settled in the country to enter into a communication with you, they acting as mediators, to obtain an honorable adjustment for both forces, in consequence of the evils which all feel are caused by the unjust war you wage; but the duty of the undersigned prohibited him from doing so, and if to-day he steps beyond the limits marked out by it, it is with the confidence inspired by the hope that there exists a definite arrangement between the two nations; for the undersigned being animated with the strongest wishes for the return of peace, it would be most painful to him not to have taken the means to avoid the useless effusion of human blood and its terrible consequences, during moments when the general peace might have been secured.

The undersigned flatters himself with this hope, and for that reason has thought it opportune to direct to you this note, which will be placed in your hands by Messrs. Julian Workman and Charles Flugo, who have voluntarily offered themselves to act as mediators. But if, unfortunately, the mentioned news should prove untrue, and you should not be disposed to grant a truce to the evils under which this unfortunate country suffers, of which you alone are the cause, may the terrible consequences of your want of consideration fall on your head. The citizens, all of whom compose the national forces of this department, are decided firmly to bury themselves under the ruins of their country, combating to the last moment, before consenting to the tyranny and ominous discretionary power of the agents of the government of the United States of North America.

This is no problem; different deeds of arms prove that they know how to defend their rights on the field of battle.

The undersigned still believes you will give a satisfactory solution to this affair, and in the mean time has the honour of offering to you the assurance of his consideration and private esteem. God and Liberty!

Head-quarters at the Angelos, January 1, 1847.   JOSÉ MA. FLORES.

The following copy of a letter, written by T. O. Larkin, Esq., late U. S. Consul at Monterey, California, is annexed to the reports of General Kearny and Captain Stockton, as part of the history of the transactions of Alta California; and also, that the suggestion of 'Mr. Larkin may be understood in reference to the rising of the Mexican population in California, of which he states—" *That this was caused more by the severe treatment they received from him,*" (the American naval commander,) " *than from any desire to change flags again!*"

City of the Angels, California, January 15, 1847.

DEAR SIR,—On a journey from Monterey to San Francisco, in November, without any escort, I was taken out of my bed at midnight, twenty-five miles from Monterey, and hurried down to this place, (four hundred miles,) on the best horses my captors could pick up on the road.

On my reaching this town, I found the whole country in arms. They had forced the American commandant and his fifty men to leave the place, and take shipping. This was caused more by the severe treatment they received from him, than from any desire to change flags again. They were not accustomed to military laws, and had revolted.

On reaching the general cuartel of this place, I was received by the second in command, who said my capture was of the utmost importance to the Californians, and that he must take every care of my safety. Visiters would be allowed to enter, with whom I could converse only in Spanish, and in presence of an officer. I found that the Mexicans and Californians watched each other as they paid their visits; even the General, a Mexican, was not allowed by the natives to be alone with me. He at one time made much exertion to talk with me alone, but two officers prevented it.

The second in command, on showing me my rooms, offered his services to me in every possible manner, and immediately sent me bedding, furniture and spirits. On learning my hours of eating, and mode and taste of my meals, his lady supplied me accordingly. The General despatched clothes for my use, offered to send my meals and money whenever I required it. During the week the Mexicans wished to send me and twenty other Americans to Sonora, thence to Mexico. [These were in the same house, but not allowed to speak with me.] I prepared for the journey, and gave the native officers to understand, that our forces would soon enter this town, and if Commodore Stockton should find we were carried out of the country, some of them must expect to go around Cape Horn. A revolution took place among them—the General had to give up his plan.

As the American forces from San Diego, under Commodore Stockton and General Kearny, and our other forces from Monterey, under Lieutenant-colonel Fremont, drew nigh to this city, the American prisoners who had families were set· at liberty one by one, (it was supposed they would be carried on the field,) before the Californians marched out to meet the American forces, on security of a friend or on parole. On the 9th, while the commodore and the natives were fighting their second battle, three miles from this, I was sent for and carried on the field. By three in the afternoon, the battle was over; the Californians were riding·in every direction backward and forward, yet not dispersed. The Americans were pursuing their way without moving to the right or the left, but in a solid square, on which good riders and fleet horses could make no impression. I rode up to the Mexican commander to know why I was sent for. After making his reasons known to me, and excuses why for two months he had been in arms, he ordered a junto of officers to decide what should be done with me. In the mean time, arrived a short proclamation from the mother-in-law of one of the chief officers, addressed to her countrymen, informing them, as they valued the safety of their families, to return me to the place they took° me from, which was done at night—the general sending me home.

On the 10th instant, our forces, under Commodore Stockton, entered the place; and· 400 of my countrymen and scores of friendly hands were made welcome. Some of the discharged prisoners had again been taken up to-day, without any loss of one of them; they are all here. Colonel Fremont and his forces have also marched into town. Every thing appears now well and peaceable. The Californians having risen since the commodore and the colonel took the country in July and August, and again given up, are satisfied with their efforts, and will hardly try again, if the troops are on the way, of which we hear. I am yours, &c., THOMAS O. LARKIN,
Late United States Consul, Monterey, California.

The following extract of a letter, written by Lieut. Theodore Talbot, is also given a place here, as containing information worthy of record : '

City of the Angels, California, January 15, 1847.
Since last I wrote you I have had an active life. Colonel Fremont left the City of the Angels in September, under command of Capt. A. H. Gillespie, 'with thirty odd riflemen, the commodore having entirely withdrawn his forces and proceeded with his squadron to San Francisco. We moved to the north, the colonel having with him only some forty men, (his old party,) the rest of the force having in part preceded us, and part been disbanded, with the exception of two small parties stationed south of the City of the Angels. I was left as military commandant of the town and jurisdiction of Santa Barbara, a pretty place lying on the ocean one hundred miles north of the City of the Angels, and the principal town between that place and Monterey. There were only nine men left with me, it being the colonel's intention to recruit at the north, and return immediately. The Prefect, the principal civil authority of the southern department, resided there, and I was left for the purpose of supporting him. My position was a very pleasant one; Santa Barbara being the residence of some of the stateliest Dons and pretty Senoras in all California. I had been here, however, but a few days when I received a correo, post haste from Captain Gillespie, bringing news of a rebellion in the south—the City of the Angels being surrounded by 500 of the Californians under arms. The courier had barely escaped with his life, and brought me Gillespie's motto seal, concealed in a cigarita, to vouch for the truth of what he told. Having warned me, he hurried on to the north to give this news to the colonel and commodore. I spent several anxious days—every moment expecting to be attacked in my barracks; hearing only through the women, who, noble and disinterested always in the hour of need, would give me such little information as they could obtain with regard to the motions of the insurgents.

Here let me remark, that nothing has surprised me so much, in my little intercourse with the Mexicans, as the humanity and charity of the women, as compared with the almost brutal ferocity of the men. You will recollect that Kendall sustains the same opinion with reference to the Santa Fé expedition.

Although my position was very precarious, I kept a firm upper lip, in order to keep down the people of Santa Barbara, which has some seventy fighting men, and several resident Mexican officers, until aid could be received from the north. I succeeded in this until the City of the Angels was taken, and Gillespie forced to capitulate. Manuel Garpis, the commander, then marched with two hundred men on Santa Barbara. They surrounded the town, and sent in a letter demanding my surrender, and guarantying our lives, &c., &c. They gave us two hours to deliberate. We had all determined not to surrender our arms; and, finding the place we then occupied untenable, with so small a force, we determined to push for the hills, (our best ground for fighting,) or die in the attempt. I accordingly marshaled my little force, and marched out of the town without opposition—those who lay on the road retreating to the main force which was on the lower side of the town. The few foreigners living in the town dared not assist me; *and the Californians, all of course, took arms against us.* Having so unexpectedly been allowed to pass their force, I camped in the hills overlooking the town, and determined to remain there a few days, and co-operate with any force which might be landed at Santa Barbara. I remained here eight days, when the Californians, having discovered my whereabouts, finally determined to route me out. Not knowing my exact position, they had divided into two or three parties; and one of them, consisting of some forty men, happened to strike upon the very spot where I was. I was aware of their coming, and had given my men orders not to fire until they were in among us. But my men were so eager to get a shot, that two of them who were posted in the arroyo or ravine, nearest the enemy, forgetting my instructions, fired just as they came marching in on us. They had fired too far for their own shots even to be effective, killing only the horse of one, and wounding the horse and grazing the hip of another of the enemy. But the Californians fled, nor would they again come within reach of our rifles, pouring a fire from their long carbines from the neighbouring hills. They sent a foreigner to me, offering to allow me to retain my arms and freedom, giving my parole of honour not to interfere farther in the war about to be waged.

I sent the man back with word that I preferred to fight. Finding I would not give up, they put fire in all round me, and succeeded in burning me out. I eluded them, however; and after lingering another day, in hopes that a force would arrive, I determined to push for Monterey. I came down on a rancho, called San Marco, where we got something to eat, for we had been starving for several days. We were also so fortunate as to find an old soldier of General Micheltorena, who was naturally inimical to the Californians. He piloted us across the coast mountain, which is here ninety miles wide, and very rugged, into the head of the Tule valley to the Lake of Buena Vista. Here I was familiar with the country, and after a month's travel, coming some 500 miles, mostly afoot, enduring much hardship and suffering, we at length effected a junction with Colonel Fremont at Monterey.

They were all very glad to see us, for they certainly thought we were all killed. In fact, the Californians had circulated that report. You must excuse me for dwelling on my little adventure; for the fact is, I suffered more from downright starvation, cold, nakedness, and every sort of privation, than in any trip I have yet had to make, and I have had some rough ones. Colonel Fremont had started from San Francisco in the ship Sterling; but after being out twenty days, and much bad weather, he was compelled to put into Monterey. I found him recruiting more men from the new emigrants, and preparing to go by land to the south. A day or two after I arrived, a part of two companies, under command of Captains Burrows and Thompson, were attacked by the Californians, eighty in number, the Americans having fifty-seven; they fought—four Americans were killed, and three Californians. Captain Burrows was among the killed. We marched to their assistance, to the mission of St. John's, from which place they were afraid to move, as they had a cavallada of 400 head of horses. We left St. John's for the south the 26th of November, and arrived at San Fernando on the 11th of January.

This place is twenty-five miles from the City of the Angels, which we heard the commodore and General Kearny, with 700 men, were in possession of. The commander of the Californians, Don Andres Pico, finding it impolitic to wage the war further, sent a deputation of his officers offering to surrender to Colonel Fremont. Their surrender was accepted, and we marched into the city on the 14th of January. The volunteer force was soon disbanded, and I will have a chance of returning home, I hope. * * * *

THEODORE TALBOT.

The difficulty which occurred in Alta California, in reference to the rightful governor under the American flag, was not only made manifest in the style and manner of the reports of the military and naval commanders; but the evidence of its existence, and of the irreconcilable character of the differences between the two commanders, has come home to the people of the United States in a variety of ways; and no doubt a set of charges preferred by either party, would bring out a masterly development of the manner in which our *"free government"* has been extended, and its blessings disseminated—and its growth encouraged and supported, (with the aid of the shackles and bayonets of General Kearny, and the cat-o'nine-tails of Captain Stockton,) in the El Dorado of North America.* The following example of what might be shown, is an extract of a letter written by Lieut. Col. John C. Fremont, and communicated by the Hon. Thomas H. Benton to the editor of the St. Louis Union newspaper, for publication:

"Both offered me the commission and post of governor—the one (Commodore Stockton) immediately to redeem his pledge of last fall; the other (General Kearny) offering to give the commission in four or six weeks. You are aware that I had been acting since last fall under a commission from Commodore Stockton. My battalion, then with me, was raised under that commission. On arriving at Los Angelos, I found Commodore Stockton in supreme command. General Kearny also told me, on the day of my arrival, that he had served under Commodore Stockton as the commander-in-chief, and did actually acknowledge him to be the governor of California. Some three or four days after my arrival, Commodore Stockton ordered me, in arranging my affairs, to take charge of the government, and to re-organize the battalion which I commanded. In the evening, General Kearny sent me a written order through his adjutant-general, forbidding me to do so. I immediately waited on the governor, who showed me a letter just received from General Kearny, requiring him forthwith to discontinue his acts and relinquish his authority as governor. Commodore Stockton exhibited to me his reply, in which he suspended General Kearny from all military command in this country. I would not decide between them, and determined to remain on my old ground. In the morning, I replied to General Kearny—recapitulating the occurrences of the last half year, and respectfully declared my intention to obey, as heretofore, the order of Commodore Stockton. When they settle the question of rank in command, I will conform. Much of the *onus* (burden) has been thrown upon me, and my situation is difficult. While they are disputing for command, (both gentlemen having gone to San Diego and Monterey), I am left here without the means of carrying on the government, with an insurrectionary people to control, with 500 volunteers who are anxious to see their families, and to whom we owe $50,000—with the border Indians in movement, and without a dollar to satisfy any demand." A postscript

---

* While at Santa Fé, General Kearny issued a proclamation granting naturalization to all of the people of New Mexico, including Negros, Indians, Mestidos, Sambos, and Mulattos. In California he seems to have considered himself equally the embodiment of the Constitution, Congress, and even government *de'facto*, under the style and title of *Dictator*, as the following, from a California newspaper, exhibits:

DECREE OF GOVERNOR KEARNY.

"I, Brig. Gen. Stephen W. Kearny, Governor of California, by virtue of authority in me vested by the President of the United States of America, do hereby grant, convey and release unto the town of San Francisco, the people, or corporate authorities thereof, all the right, title, and interest of the government of the United States, and of the territory of California, in and to the beach and water lots on the east front of said town of San Francisco, included between the points known as the Rincon and Fort Montgomery, excepting such lots as may be selected for the use of the United States government by the senior officers of the army and navy now there; provided, the said ground hereby ceded shall be divided into lots, and sold by public auction to the highest bidder, after three months' notice previously given—the proceeds of said sale to be for the benefit of the town of San Francisco.

"Given at Monterey, capital of California, this 10th day of March, 1847, and the seventy-first year of the Independence of the United States.

"STEPHEN W. KEARNY,
Brigadier-general and Governor of California."

The lands pretended to have been granted by the above *decree*, were granted to private individuals by the government of Spain, more than two hundred years ago; and, therefore, "the *right*, *title*, and interest of the United States" cannot be much; and if it was, the deed, or *decree* of General Kearny could not convey it—nor even the President himself, excepting by authority of Congress.

letter of the 19th of February, adds: "Since the date of my last, Commodore Shubrick has arrived, and with him a part of the force intended for this country. The remainder are daily expected. General Kearny has gone north, and has held a consultation with Commodore Shubrick. The result seems to be, from what I learn, that no move, which they consider as important, will be made until the pleasure of the President is known. Commodore Shubrick, as you will see by papers which I send, is, in effect, governor in the north—a fact not entirely consistent with the denial of Commodore Stockton's right," &c.

Thus has been *the beginning*, but not *the end*, of the difficulties which are to exist in the administration of the *present government* of Alta California; and the past and present is but a *speck* of the contentions and disagreements which are to disgrace the American flag and to degrade the institutions of our country, and thus to render republicanism a burlesque and freedom a mockery, so long as the unnecessary and improvident military occupation, taken by the government at Washington, of the distant and comparatively uninhabited provinces of Mexico shall be continued.

The following copy of a letter from the Secretary of War to General Kearny, announces the organization of Stevenson's California regiment:

WAR DEPARTMENT, *Washington, December* 12, 1846.

SIR,—A volunteer regiment, raised in the State of New York, engaged to serve during the war with Mexico, and to be discharged, wherever they may be, at its termination, if in a territory of the United States, has been mustered into service, and is about to embark at the port of New York, for California. This force is to be a part of your command; but, as it may reach the place of its destination before you are in a condition to subject it to your orders, the colonel of the regiment, J. D. Stevenson, has been furnished with instructions for his conduct in the mean time. I herewith send you a copy thereof, as well as a copy of the instructions of the Navy Department to the commander of the naval squadron in the Pacific; a copy of a letter to General Taylor, with a circular from the Treasury Department; a copy of a letter from General Scott to Captain Tompkins; and a copy of general regulations relative to the respective rank of naval and army officers. These, so far as applicable, will be looked upon in the light of instructions to yourself. The department is exceedingly desirous to be furnished by you with full information of your progress and proceedings, together with your opinion and views as to your movements into California, having reference as to time, route, &c. &c. Beyond the regiment under the command of Col. S. Price, and the separate battalion called for at the same time by the President from the governor of Missouri, a requisition for one regiment of infantry was issued on the 18th of July last; but the information subsequently received here induced the belief that it would not be needed, and the difficulty of passing it over the route at so late a period in the season, with the requisite quantity of supplies, &c., was deemed so great that the orders to muster it into service have been countermanded. It will not be sent. Your views as to the sufficiency of your force, and the practicability of sustaining a larger one, &c., are desired. I am, with great respect, your obedient servant,

WILLIAM L. MARCY, *Secretary of War.*

Gen. STEPHEN W. KEARNY, *Fort Leavenworth, Missouri.*

The belief seems to have prevailed with the Secretary of War, that Stevenson, with his California regiment, would have arrived in Alta California before General Kearny could have entered the country to assume the command-in-chief. But very different was the result of their movements. General Kearny arrived in Alta California on the 2d of December, 1846, and Stevenson not until the 3d of March, 1847, three full months afterwards. The company of United States Artillery, commanded by Captain Tompkins, is understood to have arrived some time previous to the date of Stevenson's arrival.

CHAPTER VIII.

General Scott's Letter to Captain Tompkins—Stevenson's Commission actually void—Mr Secretary Marcy to J. D. Stevenson—A Glance at Mexico—Its People and its Government —Her future Prospects as a Nation—Texas and Slavery, &c.

THE following is a copy of the communication of General Scott, addressed to Captain Tompkins, referred to in the letter of the Secretary of War, a copy of which is contained in the preceding chapter:

[*Confidential.*]

HEAD-QUARTERS OF THE ARMY, *Washington, June* 20, 1846.

SIR,—As the commander of a company of the 3d artillery, you have been ordered to embark with the same on board of the United States ship, the Lexington, now lying in the harbour of New York, and bound to the west coast of America.

I am now to inform you that, with your company, you are destined to act in conjunction with the United States naval forces in the Pacific against the Republic of Mexico, with which we are at war. The commander of that squadron may desire to capture and to hold certain important points, as Monterey, and towns or posts in San Francisco bay. The company under your command may be needed for both purposes, and you will, on consultation, give your co-operation.

It is not intended to place you under the orders, strictly speaking, of any naval officer, no matter how high in rank. That would be illegal, or at least without the. authority of any law; but you will be held responsible, when associated in service, whether on land or water, with any naval officer, without regard to relative rank, to co-operate in perfect harmony, and with zeal and efficiency. Great confidence is reposed in you in those respects, as also in your intelligence, judgment, temper, and prowess. See, in this connection, paragraphs 24, 25, and 26, in the old *General Regulations for the Army,* (edition of 1825,) a copy of which book I handed to you in my office.

Your condition, and that of your company, on board the Lexington, commanded by Lieutenant ———, of the navy, or other United States vessel to which you may be transferred, will be that of *passengers,* not *marines;* but in the event of the ship finding herself in action, you and the company under your command will not fail to show yourselves at least as efficient as any equal number of marines whatsoever. In such case, again, the utmost harmony, upon consultation, would be indispensable; and in no case will you fail, so far as it may depend upon your best exertions, to conciliate such harmony.

On the landing of the ordnance and ordnance stores belonging to the army, placed on board of the Lexington, you will take charge of the same, unless you should be joined for that purpose by an ordnance officer, in which case you will give him aid and assistance in that duty.

On effecting a successful landing in the enemy's country, it may be necessary, after consultation with the naval commander, as above, and with his assistance, to erect and defend one or more forts, in order to hold the conquered place or places. In such service you will be in your proper element.

It is proper that I should add, you may find on the north-west coast an army officer, with higher rank than your own, when, of course, you will report to him by letter, and, if ashore, come under his command.

It is known that you have made requisitions for all the proper supplies which may be needed by your company, for a considerable time after landing. Further supplies, which may not be sent after you from this side of the continent, you will, when ashore, in the absence of a naval force, and in the absence of a higher officer of the army, have to purchase on the other side; but always in strict conformity with regulations. On board, it is understood that your company will be subsisted from the stores of the ship or navy.

Should you not come under the orders of an army officer, or should you not be landed by the naval commander, as above, you will remain on board of the squadron, and be sent home on some ship of the same.

7   E

I need scarcely add that, afloat or ashore, you will always maintain the most exact discipline in your company, for the honour of the army and country, and never neglect to make, in the absence of an army superior, to the adjutant-general, the stated reports required by regulations, besides special reports on all subjects of interest.

WINFIELD SCOTT.

To 1st Lieut. C. Q. TOMPKINS, (now Captain,) 3d Artillery.

[Extract from the General Regulations of the Army—edition of 1825.]

ARTICLE 6.—*Relative rank and precedence of land and sea officers.*

24. The military officers of the land and sea services of the United States shall rank together as follows: 1st. A lieutenant of the navy with captains of the army. 2d. A master commandant with majors. 3d. A captain of the navy, from the date of his commission, with lieutenant-colonels. 4th. Five years thereafter with colonels. 5th. Ten years thereafter, with brigadier-generals; and 6th. Fifteen years after the date of his commission, with major-generals. But, should there be created in the navy the rank of rear-admiral, then such rank only shall be considered equal to that of major-general.

25. Nothing in the preceding paragraph shall authorize a land officer to command any United States vessel or navy yard; nor any sea officer to command any part of the army on land; neither shall an officer of the one service have a right to *demand* any compliment, on the score of rank, from an officer of the other service.

26. Land troops *serving* on board a United States vessel as marines, shall be subject to the orders of the sea officer in command thereof. Other land troops, embarked on board such vessels for transportation merely, will be considered, in respect to the naval commanders, as passengers; subject, nevertheless, to the internal regulations of the vessels.

The letter of instructions from the Secretary of War to Jonathan D. Stevenson, colonel of the California regiment, a copy of which follows, is a document important for consideration, as disclosing, in the frankest terms, the designs of the present administration of the government at Washington. In this it is disclosed, that notwithstanding the oft-repeated declaration of the President, that "every honourable effort had been used by him to avoid the war;" and that "it had not been waged with a view to conquest;" but, having been commenced by Mexico, it had been carried into the enemy's country, to be vigorously prosecuted there, with a view to obtain an honourable peace," it is therein openly declared by the Secretary of War, that in all the military operations directed that way, "the military occupation of California is the main object in view." Hence, Stevenson, and other commanders, have been instructed that "the possession and occupation" of certain military positions in Alta California "were essential to the objects in view in prosecuting the war in that quarter." The instructions of the Secretary of War state, for the advisement of his subordinate, that "there is reason to believe that California is not favourably disposed to the central government of Mexico, and will not be disposed to make a vigorous resistance to our operations in that quarter." He then says: "Should you find such to be the state of things there," "they should be made to feel that we come as deliverers;" and "their rights of person, property, and religion, must be respected and sustained." If this last pledge be sustained, the inquiry may be made—who is to be benefited by the acquisition of the Californias, Sonora, Chihuahua, and New Mexico?—every square mile of the soil of those vast territories, fit for cultivation, having long since been granted, by the Spanish or Mexican government, to individuals. Certainly not the people of the United States, who are to pay the expenses of the prosecution and consummation of the present scheme of annexation of the government at Washington. If it might be supposed that this grand scheme of annexation was consummated, let it be known, that so soon as the territories of Northern Mexico should come into the Union, the grants, which

, include its entire soil, would be bought up by land speculators of the United
States and the north of Europe, for a half or one cent per acre, and sold to
settlers for $1 and $2 per acre; but not a cent would come into the treasury
of the United States for the reimbursement of the people for the great expenses to which they had been subjected in the prosecution of the seizure,
military occupation, and annexation, of those territories. In the operation,
the poor would be made to pay to the rich—but not the rich to the government.

From the communication of instructions given by the Secretary of War to
Stevenson, it is plainly to be inferred to have been the original intention of
the government at Washington, that he should have been second in command in California; and that when General Kearny should have left, the
post of military-commandant and civil governor should have devolved
upon Stevenson. The assignment of Colonel Mason to the command in
California, places another between General Kearny and Stevenson, leaving
him in the third place of rank. But, as it seems, Stevenson will have another competitor in the person of Lieutenant-colonel Fremont, who was the
revolutionary chief of the country, and who will claim the right to govern,
as the real conqueror of the territory. This might be secured to him, in the
absence of both General Kearny, and Colonel Mason; and as for Stevenson,
he is acting under a commission which is absolutely void, it having been
issued by the governor of the state of New York, without any authority of
law; and his regiment has had no organization in accordance with any law
of Congress, or of the legislature of the state of New York; which facts
were known to the Secretary of War, at the time he despatched the expedition, and granted the following letter of instruction:

WAR DEPARTMENT, *September* 11, 1846.

SIR,—The transports having on board the regiment under your command are destined
to the Pacific, and will repair to our naval squadron now on the coast of California. Instructions, with a copy of which you are herewith furnished, have been given to the naval
commander on the station in regard to his operations; and you are directed to co-operate
with him in carrying out his plans, so far as the land forces may be needed for that purpose. Without undertaking to give specific instructions as to the movements of our forces
in that quarter—for much must be left to the judgment of the commanding officers—*it is
proper to state that the military occupation of California is the main object in view.* There
are three points deemed to be worthy of particular attention. These are, San Francisco,
Monterey, and San Diego. It is important to have possession of the bay of San Francisco,
and the country in that vicinity. The necessity of having something like a permanent and
secure position on the coast of California, and probably at this place, will not be overlooked.
Assuming that such a position will be found and selected in the bay of San Francisco, it
is expected that a fortification, such as the means at your command may enable you to con-
struct, will be erected, and that the heavy guns heretofore sent out, and those taken by the
transports, to the extent needed, will be used for its armament. This work should be designed for a two-fold object—the protection of the vessels in the bay, and the security of
the land forces. The selection of the site will be an important matter. It should be preceded by a careful examination of the place with reference to both objects, and the location
made under the advice and direction of the commanding naval officer. It may, however,
be that your first debarkation will not be at this point. The circumstances which may be
found to exist on your arrival in that region must control in this matter.

It is probable that Monterey will have been taken by our naval force, before the land
troops reach that coast, and they may be needed to hold possession of it. This place is
also to be secured by fortifications or temporary works from an attack either by sea or land.
Judging from the information we have here of what will be the state of things on your arrival on the coast of California, it is concluded that these will be found to be the important
points, *and the possession of them essential to the objects in view in prosecuting the war in that
quarter;* but the particular mention of them is by no means intended as instructions to

confine our military operations to them. As to the third place suggested, San Diego, less is known of it than the other two. Should the naval commander determine to take and hold possession of it, and need the land force, or a part of it for that purpose, you will of course yield to his views in that respect. Whatever is done upon the coast of California, or of any other part of Mexico, will require, it is presumed, the co-operation of the land and naval forces, and it is not doubted that this co-operation will be cordially rendered.

The point, or points of debarkation of the regiment under your command, should be settled as speedily as practicable after your arrival upon the Mexican coast, and the transports discharged. The land forces will, thereafter, be attended with the vessels of the squadron. The ordnance, ammunition, arms, and all descriptions of public property which are not required on shore, or cannot be safely deposited there, will be transferred to the public ships. Upon them the land forces must rely for bringing supplies, where water transportation is necessary. If the exigency of the service requires these forces to remove from one place to another on the coast, the public vessels will furnish the means of doing so.

The regiment under your command, as well as the company of Captain Tompkins, which has preceded it, is a part of General Kearny's command; but it may be that he will not be in a situation to reach you, by his orders, immediately on your debarkation. Until this is the case, yours will be an independent command, except when engaged in joint operations with the naval force.

It is not expected that you will be able to advance far into the country; nor is it advisable for you to undertake any hazardous enterprises. Until you shall fall under the command of General Kearny, your force will be mostly, if not wholly employed in seizing and holding important possessions on the sea-coast.

The government here have received information, which is deemed to be reliable, though not official, that our squadron in the Pacific had taken possession of Monterey, as early as the 6th of July last.

There is reason to believe, that California is not favourably disposed to the central government of Mexico, and will not be disposed to make a vigorous resistance to our operations in that quarter. Should you find such to be the state of things there, it will be of the greatest importance that the good will of the people towards the United States should be cultivated. This is to be done by liberal and kind treatment. *They should be made to feel that we come as deliverers. Their rights of person, property, and religion must be respected and sustained.* The greatest care must be taken to restrain the troops from all acts of license or outrage; the supplies drawn from the country must be paid for at fair prices; and, as far as practicable, friendly relations must be established. In the event of hostile resistance, your operations must be governed by circumstances; and you must use the means at your command to accomplish the objects in view—*the military occupation of the country.* It is not, however, expected that much can be done, if preparations shall have been made to resist, until the forces under General Kearny shall have entered the country.

You are directed to embrace every opportunity to communicate with this department, and to furnish it with not only a full account of your movements and operations previous to your coming under the direct command of General Kearny, but with such other information as may be useful for the department to possess in regard to conducting the war in that quarter.

Your attention is particularly directed to that portion of the instructions to the commanding officer of the squadron in the Pacific, herewith enclosed, which has reference to the joint operation of the land and naval force, and you will conform your conduct thereto.

You are also furnished with an extract from instructions to General Kearny, giving directions for the course of conduct to be pursued while in the military occupation of any portion of the enemy's country—together with a copy of a letter to General Taylor, enclosing one from the Secretary of the Treasury in regard to commercial intercourse with such parts of the enemy's ports, &c., as may be in possession of our forces. These are to be regarded as instructions to you, should you find yourself placed in the circumstances therein contemplated. You will take the earliest opportunity to make the commanding officer of the squadron in the Pacific fully acquainted with your instructions and the accompanying papers. Where a place is taken by the joint action of the naval and land forces, the naval officer in command, if superior in rank to yourself, will be entitled to make arrangements for the civil government of it, while it is held by the co-operation of both branches of the military force. All your powers, in this respect, will, of course, be devolved on General Kearny, whenever he shall arrive in California and assume the command of the volunteer regiment. As soon as practicable, you will furnish him with a copy of this communication and the other papers herewith transmitted.

Very respectfully, your obedient servant,

WILLIAM L. MARCY, *Secretary of War.*

Col. J. D. STEVENSON, *Commanding Regiment of Volunteers, Governor's Island, harbour of New York.*

It remains no longer as a supposition, that the present administration of the government at Washington have acted with a design to wrest from the government of Mexico the territories of the Californias, Sonora, Chihuahua, and New Mexico, with a view to the annexation of these enormously extensive countries to the United States—a measure as fraught with evil to ourselves as unjust to the inhabitants of Mexico. These vast territories have already been seized by American troops, and they are now technically in the military occupation of the government at Washington; and suppose that this grand scheme of annexation could be carried out, without objection or hindrance on the part of Mexico, (which, however, is a supposition not yet authorized,) what must be the inevitable result of the measure to the United States of America? Certainly nothing short of an almost immediate dissolution of the Union; or a change of the principles of our government from *republicanism* to an *aristocracy.* These immense territories could only be held and protected by a large standing army, and another army of civil officers, all dependent upon the chief executive of the Union, and thus increasing his patronage and the corruption of the federal capital. They could not receive a population from the United States in any limited time, as the states of this Union have not the inhabitants to spare. So that their early settlement could not be expected without looking to an emigration from northern Europe, whose people would be as proportionably strange to the institutions of our government as the territories they should inhabit would be foreign to our capital. A hundred years could not give the literature of the United States to Northern Mexico, nor spread the education there which is within the reach and common to the most indigent of American citizens. The greater number of eligible positions for settlement, and the best lands for cultivation, are along the coast of the Pacific and shores of the Gulf of California, upon an average of 2000 miles' distance from the seat of government of the United States—a distance which would never be travelled but by the parasites of power. The shipper, the merchant, the farmer, the mechanic, and all of business avocations, would never see Washington; and, though New Mexico, Chihuahua, Sonora, and the Californias, distant 2000 and 3000 miles from our capital, should be settled and peopled by citizens of the United States, they would become foreigners, being severed from the citizens of these states by distance, deserts, and mountains; and having a different soil and climate, and another commerce, which would never be connected with, nor beneficial to the United States, they could not be as one people with the Yankees—with one thought, one feeling, one sentiment, and of one national interest, without which no republic could be of long duration. The steamers upon the bays and rivers, the canals and canalboats, the railways and locomotives, the newspapers and the magnetic telegraphs, have kept us one people from the bay of Fundy to the Mississippi river; and the same agents can keep us one people to the valley of the Rio Grande del Norte. But beyond that they cannot go. Broad deserts and lofty and rugged sierras divide the east from the west, and art cannot unite them.

The assumption that, as the purchase of the valley of the Mississippi did but increase the power and prosperity of the Union, and that as we **can** bear the annexation of Texas, the government at Washington would be safe in the experiment, and the President and his advisers justified in extending our lines to the Pacific, would afford a like assurance of safety and justification for including the Sandwich Islands, Japan, and Tartary, if so pleased. Louisiana and Texas were neighbouring territories, and they had an interest interwoven with the Atlantic States by foreign and domestic commerce; but Northern Mexico is as foreign to us as France, and as little prepared for our institutions as France was in 1789; and the commerce of its inhabitants must be with strangers.

The magnificent scheme of conquest for annexation now being prosecuted by the government at Washington, may flatter the ambition of weak men, and tickle the acquisitiveness of dumpy and doty politicians; but statesman and sage will say, We meddle with Northern Mexico but to our own national hurt; that she can be forced into the Union but to palsy our government; and that, if she be now cast upon the bosom of liberty, she will assuredly breed a disease; and why should we deprive Mexico of all her means for national greatness? Why should the farmers, mechanics, and labouring men of the Atlantic States be taxed to the extent of millions of dollars that this great wrong may be done? that Mexico may be deprived of her northern states to be given to the refuse population of Europe, and to create an additional inducement for foreign emigration, which has already become a tax upon the industry of American citizens, and a nuisance to the country.

The continent, from the 42° of north latitude to the Isthmus of Panama, on the Pacific coast, and encircling the west and south-westerly sides of the Gulf of Mexico, was once a vice-royalty of Spain. The people of that country had witnessed the successful struggle of our forefathers for political liberty, and they saw us experimenting with equal success, with a popular form of government, and they aimed to practise what we had experimented, and in 1810, they struck for the same glorious principles for which our forefathers fought;* but, perhaps, they struck too soon. Their cause had but little prosperity until the Treaty of Ghent and the Peace of Paris deprived many officers of the American and European armies of employment, who flocked to the Mexican standard, to do battle in the cause of liberty. As English cupidity had afflicted the British American colonies, which now compose a part of the states of this Union, with the curse of domestic slavery, so had the Spanish grandees who had domiciled themselves in Mexico doubly cursed their vice-royalty with the same evil. The slaveholders of Mexico were the loyal supporters of the Spanish authority in the viceroyalty, and the patriots of the country, as a measure of justice to themselves, and of injury and hurt to their enemies, declared an abrogation of the law of slavery which had prevailed in their country; and freed slaves with foreign officers became good material to fight *the battles of liberty*. But when these were won, the foreign officers mainly returned to their homes in other lands, and the freed slaves were not found best fitted for citizens; and the energies of the people were fatally weakened by a suicidal act of the people, who aimed at their annihilation, and the government of Mexico, who consented to the expulsion from their territories of all nativeborn Spaniards. These formed the most able and enlightened of their inhabitants; and though, not like the Jews of Egypt, seeking to go, their absence,

---

* The Revolution in Mexico was commenced, in 1810, by Don Miguel Hidalgo, a priest of Dolores, a small town in the Intendencia of Guanajuato; associated with whom were three Spanish military officers, Allende, Aldama, and Abasolo.

when thrust out, did the Mexican nation more injury than did the fleeing of Moses's band to the country of Pharaoh. The generations of the freed slaves and, the Indians were too numerous for the whites. These facts, combining with the farther one, that a climate of extraordinary salubrity, and a soil over-fruitful, exist as a natural and never-failing encouragement to idleness and vagabondism. These are the ingredients which have deteriorated from the character of the Mexican people, and given apparent failure to their experiment in free self-government, and thrown them back a century behind the present age of art, science and improvement. Mexico is too weak; her debility rendered by these causes is too great to allow her to rise, unaided by encouragement and assistance from abroad. The agents of foreign industry and improvement must be brought in among them, and the genius of invention be allowed to take its lead, and her inferior races must give place to the superior, or her head can never rise among the nations of the earth. But these breeds of the African and the Aztec races must have ground to retire upon, or they cannot go. Deprive Mexico of her northern provinces, and she remains depressed under her burden of Negros, Indians, Mulattos, Mestidos, and Sambos, breeds of men who are doomed by nature to ignorance and stupidity, and whose presence, in their present redundancy of numbers, does but clog the wheels of their national advancement, shut out the light of genius and science, and render futile and unstable all forms of free government, by furnishing the ready means and willing instruments for political dissension, revolt and revolution. Let Mexico scatter this part of her population in Northern Mexico, and its influence is neutralized, its power lost, and its ability to do the nation hurt will exist no more. If, however, she is to be deprived of her unsettled territories, her hopes of national greatness are blasted, and of regeneration denied. With the millions of her inferior races compressed within her smaller territories, not assisting but cramping her energies, republican institutions would be found insufficient for the ignorance of these and the consequent supineness of the whites, and necessity would give the rule to despotism or monarchy. One of the vital means for the regeneration of Mexico, is commerce; and deprived of her northern provinces, Mexico will be shorn of her means for commercial prosperity, *as they contain her only good harbours*.

Had Mexico remained a vice-royalty of Spain, the government at Washington would not have plunged our country into a war with that monarchy, and, perhaps, with all Europe, with a view to the dismemberment of her territories; and now, because the Mexican people, at the instigation of our government, assisted by our citizens, have made a feeble effort to imitate us in the establishment and maintenance of a free government, shall we despoil her, that ourselves may be ruined with the appropriation of the plunder?

There is another problem embraced in the project under consideration. Will the industrious, hard-working, labouring people of the Northern and Middle States, who are the great consumers, and, consequently, the great tax-payers of the Union, and from the sweat of whose brows has ever been drawn the means for the support of our national government, consent to have their burden of taxes increased in a three or fourfold, to defray the expenses of seizing and maintaining a military occupation of the territories of a sister republic, that "the area of slavery may be increased," and a new market opened for the sale of men, women, and children? Or, will the people of the slave states, think ye, fellow-citizens of the land of the white rain, allow their territories to be environed with a cordon of free states,

whose soil shall be parcelled out to and owned by those who help themselves and do their own bidding? Or, will they not rather plant the bonds-
men throughout those territories, whose "*soil and climate are peculiarly
adapted to slave labour?*"

CHAPTER IX.

*Opinion of the Hon. James Buchanan of the Wilmot Proviso—His Appeal to the Democracy
of Pennsylvania—The Question of Slavery in California reviewed—36° 30', or the Missouri
Compromise—The Policy of the South, and the Motive for a Slave Market—Emigrants to
California and Northern Mexico.*

IF it be allowed by our code of morals, and held consistent with the light
of the age, that the priest in the pulpit may lie, in order to gain credence
for revelation; that the counsellor who appears in the law court of the people may clothe falsehood in the habiliments of truth, and give her the tongue
of philosophy, that his client's cause may seem just; and that a wise statesman may put forth a fallacy, that his particular policy of government shall
find favour with the people of his country, then may there be an apology
granted to the Hon. James Buchanan, Secretary of State of the United
States, for the number of bare-headed misstatements of fact which he has
crowded into a communication (1.) recently addressed by him to a number
of citizens of Berks county, Pennsylvania.*

" The question of slavery," writes Mr. Secretary Buchanan, " in one of its
ancient aspects, has been recently revived, and threatens to convulse the country:" and then, after giving words of advice to the democracy of Pennsylvania,
he continues: " *Northern Democrats are not expected to approve slavery in
the abstract;* but they owe it to themselves, as they value the Union, and
all of the political blessings which bountifully flow from it, *to abide the compromise of the Constitution, and to leave the question, where that instrument has left it,* TO THE STATES WHEREIN SLAVERY EXISTS:"† and then, in

---

* The extravagance of the averments which this communication contains, will appear
much less to diminish the character of the writer for intelligence, when viewed in connection with the following declaration by which they are prefaced:
" *It is a long time since,*" says Mr. Secretary Buchanan, " *any state election* [referring to
the gubernatorial election of the State of Pennsylvania, then to be held in October, 1847,]
*has involved such important consequences for the democracy of the Union, as the approaching
election for Governor of Pennsylvania. On its results may probably depend the ascendency
of the democracy of the Union for years to come;*" but this presents no favourable comment
upon the Secretary's character for political honesty.
It was neither the intention nor the appropriate office of the writer to go into a canvass
of the fears of Mr. Secretary Buchanan, for the loss of the State of Pennsylvania from the
democratic galaxy, which he seems to have shadowed forth as then likely to result from an
estrangement of a portion of the democracy. But, taking his letter in question as declaratory of the policy of President Polk and his advisers in reference to matters of the highest
national importance; and as their avowed policy appears to be in opposition to the principles of justice and humanity, threatening the stability of the government of the United
States, and detrimental to the best interest of the American people, it seems to have been
worthy of an elucidation.
† Let the reader bear in mind that it is not the regulation of their local matters of slavery
which Mr. Secretary Buchanan insists should be left " to the states wherein slavery exists;"
but the whole matter of the *conquest*, and *annexation* to this Union, of a vast territory, and

reference to the further acquisition of territory and the creation of new states, and after declaring that, " under the Missouri Compromise, slavery was *forever prohibited* north of 36° 30'; and" that " south of that parallel the question was left to the people," he writes—" and in my opinion, the harmony of the states, *and even the security of the Union itself*, require that the line of the Missouri Compromise *should be extended to any new territory which we may acquire from Mexico!*"

Slavery, " in its ancient aspect," is one of hateful features to the democracy of the north. because it is viewed as a blight upon the prosperity of the country, and an institution which, in principle, is at war with the genius of free government; and with no other, nor with more pleasant features, can the question ever be revived; but there is no terror in the convulsion which it threatens—*unless the democracy of the north shall prove traitors to their own principles!* As for " the compromise of the Constitution," it is to be argued that that compromise embraced no territory not at the time of the creation of the instrument a part and parcel of the territory of this Union; and that it is in no manner binding in reference to territory subsequently acquired, and which had no representation in the Convention by which the Constitution was framed. The compromise was such only between the thirteen original states.* Nor was the Missouri Compromise a

---

one as extensive as the entire of the original thirteen states, and the construction of the same into a great slave market, which shall be the means of keeping slavery in parts of this Union where it would otherwise soon cease to exist for the want of a motive for its continuance. He *modestly* asks the citizens of Pennsylvania to give their lives, their national character, their right to be heard in the national councils, and their public treasures, into the keeping, arrangement, and disposal of their neighbours—the slaveholders of the South! (where, as he contends, the Constitution has placed the question of slavery;) and that they should so vote, in 1847, that California, a country now acknowledged to be free, may be obtained by *their blood* and *their money*, to be made *a land of slaves!* and unless slavery be admitted to California, (and in aid of which he solicits the votes of the democracy of Pennsylvania,) Mr. Secretary Buchanan is of the opinion that the Union is insecure: and assumes that, for our blood-bought institutions there is now no safety except in the manacles of slaves! As Mr. Secretary Buchanan puts it to the Pennsylvanians—a vote for Mr. Shunk would be a vote for slavery in California; *and who,* BUT SLAVES, *would vote for chains and slavery?*

* The following is a copy of *Clause* 3, *Sec.* 2, *Art.* 4, of the Constitution of the United States:—No *person held to service or labour* in one state, under the laws thereof, escaping into another, shall, in consequence of any law or regulation therein, be discharged from such service or labour, but shall be delivered up upon claim of the party to whom such service or labour may be due.

Again: *Clause* 3, *Sec.* 2, *Art.* 1, of the Constitution of the United States, is as follows:—Representatives [in Congress] and direct taxes shall be apportioned among the several states which may be included within this Union, according to their respective numbers, *which shall be determined by adding to the whole number of free persons,* including those bound to service for a term of years, and excluding Indians not taxed, *three-fifths of all other persons.*

The word *slavery* is not mentioned in the Constitution of the United States; and the preceding are the copies of each and every clause of the Constitution which can be deemed to have reference to slavery. The *first* is a provision introduced, *very properly,* with a view to prevent the free states from interfering with the internal regulations of the slave states, as well as to secure to the people of the slave states the possession of their *property,* invested in slaves. The *second* is a provision giving to the inhabitants of the slave states a representation in Congress for their *property.* These were immunities which the people of the Southern states could not have claimed as a right, and therefore they were matters clearly of *compromise;* and as *clearly* have no manner of reference to, or bearing upon the subject of the conquest of territory, or the extension of slavery. It is not true that the Constitution, by its compromise, has left the question of *conquest,* and of *slavery* as it may be connected with the admission of foreign territory into the Union, " *to the states wherein slavery*

8

binding compact, that it should now determine the fate of territory (as to the existence of slavery therein) not yet acquired ; (2.) if the force of that compromise, in any direction, be not impeached by the principles of our government, which do not permit the acts of one Congress to bind the proceedings of a succeeding one; each Congress being supposed to represent the opinions and to carry out the wishes of the people, *as they exist for the time being.* The government of this Union was reared upon a declaration, declaring it to be the inherent right of the people, whenever any form of government becomes destructive of their just rights, to alter or to abolish it, and to institute a new one, based upon such principles as shall seem most likely to effect their safety and happiness; and the constitutional authority by which every national legislature is convoked, could have no existence without a recognition of the right of an existing Congress to change, modify, or abolish the acts of any Congress by which it may have been preceded. Nor would the advocates of the slave interest be slow in reminding the people of the Union of this principle of the government, if it should become their interest to plant slavery in any territory north of 36° 30'.*

That " northern Democrats," as well as the northern people generally, " do not approve of slavery in the abstract," is most true ! (Nor are they favourably disposed to the acquisition of territory by conquest.†) But a very,

---

exists ;" and the assumption is an insult to the intelligence of the freemen of Pennsylvania, and seems to have been put forth, NOT for those who *can write and read for themselves.*

* It is certainly difficult to view the letter of Mr. Secretary Buchanan in any other light than as *an official declaration* in behalf of the present administration of the government at Washington, against the principles of *the Wilmot Proviso,* and in favour of the schemes which they have openly and boldly prosecuted, for the seizure of the territories of Northern Mexico, with a view to establish therein *an extensive slave market* for the benefit of the slave-owners of the Southern States of this Union. Such seems to be the only construction which it can bear ; and upon this Mr. Buchanan (most extraordinarily !) supplicates the people of Pennsylvania to vote for Mr. Shunk for Governor, at their election in 1847, not on account of any benefit which might accrue to those people by means of his election to the gubernatorial chair, but because his (Mr. Shunk's) defeat might bring failure to their great scheme for " extending the area of slavery" to the shores of the Pacific Ocean ; and he (Mr. Secretary Buchanan) would have the voters of Pennsylvania believe that the American people can have no expansion of their lines without a corresponding spread and growth of *slavery ;* that the keystone of the democratic arch they boast is *slavery,* and that, without *slavery,* it must fall ; and that there are no bands to the Union but those which have been wrought by *slavery.*

> " Slaves in the ancient Aztec's land !
> We tell thee, JAMES BUCHANAN, never—
> Her rocky hills and iron strand
> *Are free, and shall be free forever ;*
> Her surf shall wear those strands away—
> Her rocky hills in dust shall moulder,
> Ere Slavery's hateful chains shall lay
> *Unbroken* on a Mexic shoulder."

† The following is a copy of a paragraph contained in a letter addressed by the late Hon. Silas Wright, while governor of the state of New York, under date of " Albany, July 7, 1846," to the Hon. William L. Marcy, Secretary of War of the United States : " If it be designed to make our present war with Mexico, one of conquest and appropriation of any part of the territory professedly and indisputably hers, *I think the design a mistaken one ;* I am, as decidedly as any man in the country, for prosecuting this war with all the requisite vigour and energy necessary to bring it to an early and successful termination ; and for so prosecuting it as well within the conceded territory and jurisdiction of Mexico, as within the United States, or the territory in dispute between the two countries. But I would cause it to be constantly and distinctly understood, that I did not invade 'he.

important cause, in aid of the principles of the people of the Northern States, which has occasioned slavery to be expelled from their territories, is the high price at which the lands in those states are held. This is all that *soil* has had to do with breaking the chains of slavery : *climate* and *productions* nothing ! Yet, Mr. Secretary Buchanan promulgates the assurance to his friends in Pennsylvania, that " neither the soil, the climate, nor the productions of that portion of California, south of 36° 30', NOR, INDEED, OF ANY PORTION OF IT, NORTH OR SOUTH, IS ADAPTED TO SLAVE LABOUR ; *and, besides, every facility would be there afforded to the slave to escape from his master.*"

Upon lands which cost from $50 to $100 per acre, (except they be good lands for the production of sugar,) slave labour cannot be profitably applied. Of good sugar lands, (except in Mexico and the West India Islands,) there are no considerable quantity on this continent ; and for all other products, lands must not cost more than from $1 to $6 per acre, to allow a proper return for slave labour ; and the lands of California will not obtain higher prices than these for many years to come ; and in California, Sonora, and New Mexico, as good wheat, corn, and tobacco can be raised as are produced in Maryland, Virginia, Kentucky, or Tennessee ; and as good cotton as Alabama or Mississippi can produce, may also be grown in California ; and as fine cattle and horses as can be raised in Arkansas, Missouri, or any other of the slave states. As for climate, California is as mild, up to its north line of 42°, as Virginia or Kentucky ; and as for " slave property being utterly insecure in any part of California," as supposed by Mr. Secretary Buchanan, the fact would be exactly the reverse. California would be the very country from which *the slave could not escape,* as from thence they would have no Ohio, New York, New Jersey, or Pennsylvania to run to ; and instead of the few blacks who now inhabit California, and who are assumed now to be free, being sufficient to keep slavery from the territory, it is far more probable that they would get their own wrists fitted to the shackles by *the treasure-hunting whites !* and thus become the companions, in slavery, of their emigrating brethren from the Southern states of the Union. The question turns not upon the present population of California, which is now merely nominal, *but that which is to be given to the country.*

It is a fact too well known throughout the United States, to admit of question, that the rise in the value of lands in many of the Southern states, (without a corresponding advance in the price of produce, which has not taken place in any of the states,) has rendered slave labour entirely unproductive, and slave property there of no value, except for their increase. If the slaves can produce enough for their own food and to pay the interest of the investment for lands, the slaveholder is satisfied, looking to *the income from the sale of young slaves* for his remuneration and support. It, therefore, becomes apparent, that if there had not been found a market for the increase of slaves, formed by the incorporation of the Mississippi territory into this Union, there had not remained, at this day, a slave in any one of the original thirteen states ; and, now, however approved may have been the policy for the extension of " the area of freedom " to the south, it is certain that " the area of slavery " has been greatly extended therewith ;

territory of Mexico for the purpose of conquest and appropriation, and that so far as the question of boundary is involved, I should be at all times ready to make a treaty, establishing the same boundary which we claimed at the commencement of the war."

From the preceding, it will be seen that the late Hon. Silas Wright was for—" NO MEXICAN TERRITORY."

and that it will grow in dominion as our country shall grow in extent south of **36° 30′**. The commerce of the Mississippi may have embraced advantages sufficient to justify the annexation of Louisiana with all its extension of slavery. But this forms no precedent for despoiling Mexico of California, as the commerce of the Pacific coast must ever be against the commerce of the Atlantic states of the Union.

It is proper that the people of the Northern states should abide the *compromise* of the Constitution ; and there have been presented no good reasons on which to found a belief, that the people of the Northern states, (excepting only a few fanatical abolitionists,) are not disposed to account as valid the provisions of the Constitution, and remain content with the guarantee which that instrument has given to slavery. They are willing to abide the *compromise* of the Constitution ; but this does not bind them to surrender their right to be heard in the councils of the nation, or deny them the liberty to object to the acquisition of further *privileged territory,* by conquest or otherwise : nor will they concede, to party obligation, the power to bind them to the slaveholding interest of the south, and to tie their hands so that they may not protect their own interests as American freemen.*

Mr. Secretary Buchanan declares that "a storm is approaching"—and with advice to the democracy, to be prepared for the same, he writes : "Their [the democratic party] best security in the hour of danger, is to cling fast to *their time-honoured principles ;*" id est, to the principles of southern slavery ! Again he writes : "*A sacred regard for the Federal Constitution, and for the reserved rights of the states, is the immovable basis on which the party* [democratic] *can alone safely rest.*" Hence, according to Mr. Secretary Buchanan, the party called *democratic* has no safety for its existence except by its adhesion to *southern slavery* and *unequal representation ;* the slave states being allowed a representation in Congress for their *property,* which was a privilege granted to them by the Constitution as *a compromise,* in order to bring into the Union the entire states of the Confederation, whose people, shoulder to shoulder with those of the Northern states, had battled for political liberty in the Revolutionary struggle of the country. But the *compromise* of the Constitution as herein-before premised, by no means included the acquisition of immense territories by conquest, or otherwise, to be appropriated to slave labour ; and to be invested with the immunities of the *compromise* of the Constitution. The fathers of the north could make no *such compromise* for their children—no agreement in favour of slavery beyond the then actual limits of the states— or compact which should bind the then unborn millions of freemen of America, in reference to unacquired territory !

"It is *morally impossible,*" continues Mr. Secretary Buchanan, "that a majority of the emigrants to that portion of the territory, (California, south of 36° 30′,) which will be chiefly composed of our fellow-citizens from the Eastern, Middle and Western states, *will ever re-establish slavery in its limits.*" If this be true, why object to the Wilmot Proviso, which only prohibits that which Mr. Secretary Buchanan declares cannot exist by a moral impossibility ? But there is reason to suspect the validity of Mr. Secretary Buchanan's assurances ; as Mr. John C. Calhoun, in his place in

---

* The democracy of Pennsylvania are told, by Mr. Secretary Buchanan, that to differ with the present administration of the government at Washington, on the question of slavery is *to "distract, and possibly to destroy the democratic party."* This is a phase of the matter proper to be viewed by *real* democrats ; and for the consideration of such the suggestion is presented.

the United States Senate, during the last session of Congress declared himself opposed to the *Wilmot Proviso*,* because it would, in effect, as he alleged, exclude the people of the Southern states from California, *or any new territory which we might acquire from Mexico*, and give it exclusively to emigrants from the non-slaveholding states; and the whole course of the administration has been bent to keep away the people of " the Eastern, Middle and Western states," while they have so ordered the measures of government as to show the country of Mexico to the slaveholders of the south, (3.) and to insure them, if possible, the possession of the same.

NOTES TO CHAPTER IX.
(1.) OPINION OF THE HON. JAMES BUCHANAN OF THE WILMOT PROVISO.

GENTLEMEN,—I have been honoured by the receipt of your kind invitation to unite with the democracy of Old Berks in their Harvest Home celebration, to be held at Reading, on Saturday, the 28th instant. I should esteem it both a pleasure and a privilege to be present on that interesting occasion: it is, therefore, with regret I have to inform you, that my public duties during the present week will render this impossible.

I rejoice to observe that the glorious democracy of " Old Berks" are buckling on their armour, and preparing for the approaching contest. It is long since any state election has involved such important consequence for the democracy of the Union, as the approaching election for governor of Pennsylvania. On its result may probably depend the ascendency of the democracy of the Union for years to come. Hence our democratic brethren of other states are witnessing the contest with intense anxiety. The field is a fair one; our candidate well-tried, able, and honest; and he has been regularly nominated by the party. Should he be defeated, the attempt will be vain to explain the decision of the ballot-boxes, in any other manner than by admitting that the Whigs have the majority. Our candidate for canal commissioner is, also, above all reproach, both personally and politically, and is eminently qualified for the duties of that important office. If, under such circumstances, the democratic keystone should give way, there is great danger that the arch may tumble into pieces. In this contest, emphatically, he that is not for us is against us. I do not apprehend defeat, unless our wily foe should first lull us into security by making no extraordinary public efforts; and then, at the eleventh hour, quietly steal a march upon us, as they have done in some other states. Our vigilance ought to be constantly on the alert, until the moment of victory.

The question of slavery in one of its ancient aspects, has been recently revived, and threatens to convulse the country. The democratic party of the Union ought to prepare themselves in time for the approaching storm. Their best security in the hour of danger, is to cling fast to their time-honoured principles. A sacred regard for the federal Constitution, and for the reserved rights of the states, is the immovable basis on which the party can alone safely rest. This has saved us from the inroads of abolition. Northern democrats are not expected to approve slavery in the abstract; but they owe it to themselves, as they value the Union, and all the political blessings which bountifully flow from it, to abide by the compromises of the Constitution, and leave the question, where that instrument has left it, to the states where slavery exists. Our fathers have made this agreement with their

---

* The following is a copy of the *amendment* to the *Three Million Bill*, (passed at the session of Congress of 1847,) introduced by Mr. David Wilmot, of Pennsylvania, in the United States House of Representatives:

Provided 'further, That there shall be neither slavery nor involuntary servitude in any territory on the continent of America, which shall hereafter be acquired by or annexed to the United States, by virtue of this appropriation, or in any other manner whatever, except for crimes whereof the party shall have been duly convicted; *Provided always*, that every person escaping into such territory from whom labour or service is lawfully claimed in any one of the United States, such fugitive may be lawfully claimed and conveyed out of said territory to the power claiming his or her labour or service.

The first vote on this amendment was—For it, 115; against it, 106; absent, 6. For it from slave states, 1; against it from free states, 18.

F

brethren of the south; and it is not for the descendants of either party, in the present generation, to cancel this solemn compact. The abolitionists, by their efforts to annul it, have arrested the natural progress of emancipation, and done great injury to the slaves themselves.

After Louisiana was acquired from France by Mr. Jefferson, and when the state of Missouri, which constituted a part of it, was about to be admitted into the Union, the Missouri question arose, and in its progress threatened the dissolution of the Union. This was settled by the men of the last generation, as other important and dangerous questions have been settled, in a spirit of mutual concession. Under the Missouri Compromise, slavery was "for ever prohibited" north of 36° 30'; and south of this parallel the question was left to be decided by the people. Congress, in the admission of Texas, following in the footsteps of their predecessors, adopted the same rule; and in my opinion, the harmony of states, and even the security of the Union itself, require that the line of the Missouri Compromise should be extended to any new territory which we may acquire from Mexico.

I should entertain the same opinion, even if it were certain this would become a serious practical question; but that it never can be thus considered, must be evident to all who have attentively examined the subject.

Neither the soil, the climate, nor the productions of that portion of California south of 36° 30', nor indeed of any portion of it, north or south, is adapted to slave labour; and, besides, every facility would be there afforded to the slave to escape from his master. Such property would be utterly insecure in any part of California. It is morally impossible, therefore, that a majority of the emigrants to that portion of the territory south of 36° 30', which will be chiefly composed of our fellow-citizens from the Eastern, Middle, and Western states, will ever re-establish slavery within its limits. In regard to New Mexico, east of the Rio Grande, the question has been already settled by the admission of Texas into the Union.

Should we acquire territory beyond the Rio Grande, and east of the Rocky Mountains, it is still more improbable that a majority of the people of that region would consent to re-establish slavery. They are, themselves, in a large proportion, a coloured population; and among them, the negro does not socially belong to a degraded race.

The question is, therefore, not one of practical importance! Its agitation, however honestly intended, can produce no effect but to alienate the people of different portions of the Union from each other; to excite sectional divisions and jealousies; and to distract and possibly destroy the democratic party, on the ascendency of whose principles and measures depends, as I firmly believe, the success of our grand experiment of self-government.

Such have been my individual opinions, openly and freely expressed, ever since the commencement of the present unfortunate agitation; and of all places in the world, I prefer to put them on record before the incorruptible democracy of Old Berks. I, therefore, beg leave to offer you the following sentiment:—

The Missouri Compromise:—Its adoption in 1820 saved the Union from threatened convulsion. Its extension in 1848 to any new territory which we may acquire, will secure the like happy result.   Yours, very respectfully,

JAMES BUCHANAN.

(2.) THE MISSOURI COMPROMISE.

The following is a copy of the section of the act of Congress, (passed in 1820,) for the admission of the state of Missouri to the Union, which is now denominated the "Missouri Compromise:"

Sec. 8. Be it further enacted, That in all that territory ceded by France to the United States, under the name of Louisiana, which lies north of thirty-six degrees, and thirty minutes north latitude, not included within the limits of the state contemplated by this act, slavery and involuntary servitude, otherwise than in the punishment of crimes, whereof the parties shall have been duly convicted, shall be, and is hereby, for ever prohibited: Provided always, That any person escaping into the same, from whom labour or service is lawfully claimed, in any state or territory of the United States, such fugitive may be lawfully reclaimed and conveyed to the person claiming his or her labour or service, as aforesaid.

(3.) THE VOLUNTEERS.

By virtue of the provisions of the Act of Congress, approved May 13, 1846, declaring the existence of the war with the Republic of Mexico, the President of the United States, immediately after the passage of the said Act of Congress, made a call upon the governors of the several states for the organization of quotas of volunteers for service in the war with Mexico, according to the ratio of population. But, after the organization of their respective quotas in the Middle and Eastern states, (at the private expenses of the citizens tendering their services as volunteers,) in pursuance of the call made by the government at Washington, the volunteers from those states were rejected, while more than the quotas from the Western and slave states were received. *Only two regiments of volunteers, amounting to about 1500 men, have been accepted from New York and the six New England States,* which together embrace a population of 4,653,790; while the two states of Kentucky and Tennessee, with a united free population of only 1,243,721, *have been permitted to have ten regiments of volunteers in service, amounting to about* 10,000 men. The last division of volunteers called for by the government at Washington embraced two regiments from Tennessee, two from Kentucky, and one from Indiana; four regiments from slave states, and one from a Western State.

The first division of volunteers mustered into the United States service for the prosecution of the war with Mexico, was composed of ten regiments and two companies from Western states, amounting to 8500 officers and men; thirteen regiments, one squadron and one company from slave states, amounting to 13,084 officers and men; *and not a regiment nor company from the Middle or Eastern states.* The distribution of the officers in the *ten regiments* of regulars, authorized to be raised by the Act of Congress, approved February 11, 1847, were disposed of by the President with equal partiality to the slave-holders. Of the thirty posts of the field officers, sixteen (more than one half) were bestowed upon slave-holders, three were army promotions, four from Middle states, two from Eastern states, and five from Western states, as follows; (slaveholders in *italics:*)

3D REG'T DRAGOONS.	1ST REG'T VOLTIGEURS.
Edward G. W. Butler, Col. of La.	*Timothy P. Andrews, Col. of D. C.*
Thomas P. Moore, Lt. Col. of Ky.	Joseph E. Johnston, Lt. Col. Army.
William H. Polk, Major, of Tenn.	*George A. Caldwell, Major, of Ky.*

COLONELS OF INFANTRY.

Truman B. Ransom, of Vt.	*John W. Tibbatts, of Ky.*
Robert E. Temple, of N. Y.	Albert G. Ramsey, of Penn.
Robert M. Echols, of Ga.	*Louis D. Wilson, of N. C.*
William Trousdale, of Tenn.	George W. Morgan, of Ohio.

LIEUTENANT-COLONELS OF INFANTRY.

Millege L. Bonham, of S. C.	Henry L. Webb, of Ill.
Jones M. Withers, of Ala.	*William M. Graham, of Va.*
John J. Fay, of N. Y.	Joshua Howard, of Mich.
Paul O. Herbert, of La.	George H. Talcott, Army.

MAJORS OF INFANTRY.

Thomas H. Seymour, of Conn.	Ralph G. Norvell, of Ind.
John C. Hays, of Texas.	Edwin W. Morgan, of Penn.
Jeremiah Clements, of Ala.	Frederick D. Mills, of Iowa.
John H. Savage, of Tenn.	Fowler Hamilton, Army.

Has this course of the government at Washington, in the distribution of the volunteer force employed against Mexico, been dictated by motives of economy? Certainly not; because troops can be conveyed from New York, or Boston, to Vera Cruz, or Matamoras, at less expense to the government than from New Orleans. Is it because southern volunteers are more brave than the descendants of the heroes of Bunker-hill and Saratoga, or that they can better endure the fatigues of the march and the severities of the climate? It is not so alleged nor shown; because the rank and file of the regular army are almost exclusively made up of recruits enlisted in the Middle and Eastern states, and the following, from a newspaper, may be evidence in point:

"A Tampico letter, of the 17th of August, says that the Louisiana regiment in that place, under command of Colonel De Russey, left their homes, a few months ago, 1000 strong, and, of this number, not more than 200 appeared on parade on the 16th. The diseases of the climate had brought about this sad change in the regiment."

By the adjutant-general's annual report, made under date of "November 26, 1845," it is shown that the number of recruits enlisted for the *general service* in the year ending the

30th of September, 1845, was 1365; and that of these 628 were enlisted in the state of
New York, 258 in Pennsylvania, 150 in Massachusetts, four in Rhode Island, seventy-four
in Maryland, 248 in Kentucky, one in North Carolina, and two in Washington, D. C.
Thus it is shown, that, of the 1365 of the rank and file of the regular army enlisted during
the twelve months preceding September 30, 1845, there were recruited 1190 in the Eastern and Middle states, *and but 25 in the slave states.* By the same officer's annual report,
made under date of " December 5, 1846," it is shown that the number of recruits enlisted
for the *general service* in that year was 2576; and that, of this number, 1786 were obtained from the Eastern and Middle states, (New York furnishing 1054, and Pennsylvania
351,) and 790 from the Western states, *and only 411 from the slave states.* Thus is exhibited the fact, that the Eastern and Middle states are permitted to furnish the rank and
file of the regular army, (who are supposed to come from the uneducated and humbler class
of the people,) while the South furnishes the officers; and that with southern officers for the
regular army, the government at Washington have added the southern corps of volunteers,
with their slave-holding officers, (the rank and file of the volunteers being deemed of a
better class of people than those of the regulars;) and these are sent to Mexico to acquire
a knowledge of, and interest in, that country, and to gain an eclat and a fame which shall
give them a popularity with the people, and an influence in future Congresses to be used
for the support of the interest of the slave-holders of the Southern states of this Union;
while northern volunteers are excluded from the service, that the recruiting ground for
the regular army may not be interfered with; but more particularly that the non-slave-
holders may not be permitted to see and admire the soil destined for slave-labour, nor be
enabled to acquire, in the prosecution of the war with Mexico, a knowledge of that country, and a fame and popularity which might be used against " the extension of the area of
slavery."

Few of the north, it is feared, have ever properly considered the effect of the monopoly
of office by the slave-holders of the south; and, therefore, it is hoped that this may arrest
their attention. It is not merely because of the fact that the government at Washington
has bestowed more than a fair proportion of army offices upon the inhabitants of slave
states, that the freemen of the north make their complaint, but for the reason that the
military appointments bring civil ones, and the fame which they acquire in the field of
glory, (from which the inhabitants of the free states are almost entirely excluded, unless
they go as common soldiers to be *numbered*, not *named*, in the bulletin, and to have their
bodies burned in stacks, or buried in pits,) gains them a political strength which they use
to the prejudice of the state rights, and rights of individuals of the north. A plain citizen,
however honest, and wise, and capable, but with his name unassociated with deeds of arms,
and not adorned with victories gained, cannot keep himself long in place or in favour with
his people; but, *military fame* forms a shield, or defence, behind which a man may retire,
and, with his wounds obtained in battle, cover his misdeeds, and for them claim the favour
of the people; and, by long continuance in the houses of the national legislature, members
acquire a strength and influence in the councils of the nation which nothing but frequent
re-elections can give. All this is too much to be claimed for the south by virtue of the
" *compromise of the Constitution.*"

The appointment of General Washington, as commander-in-chief of the armies of the
revolution, was *a compromise* with slavery, and by his military command came the office
of President; and he appointing Jefferson, Madison, and Monroe, to office, and putting
them in the way to be kept continually before the people of the Union in some place of
the federal government, secured to them, in turn, the office of President; and, without
their military fame, neither Jackson, nor Harrison had ever found himself chief magistrate
of this Union; and it has not been because the slave states produce better or more able
men than the free states of the Union, that the *slave dominion* has been permitted to furnish
eight of the *eleven* Presidents, and to have the presidential office filled by their citizens forty-
eight years out of *fifty-six*, but by the general monopoly of office, both civil and ▮▮▮
The acquisition and annexation of the Californias and New Mexico will but in▮▮▮
wrongs complained of, and nourish the institution of slavery, and encourage ▮▮▮
gration to an extent which has never yet been apprehended. These evils, h▮▮▮▮▮▮y
all be abated by taking NO MEXICAN TERRITORY, which ought to be the policy of
the federal government.